The Consumers' Guide

to

Investment

Real Estate

How to Avoid Common Traps and Problems and Learn to Make REAL Money in Real Estate Investment

by

Jim Toner

The Consumers' Guide to Investment Real Estate

How to Avoid Common Traps and Problems and Learn to Make REAL Money in Real Estate Investment

Jim Toner
Copyright ©2016

Printed in the United States of America
Cover design:
ISBN: 978-0-9912520-1-5

The Consumers' Guide to Investment Real Estate:
How to Avoid Common Traps and Problems and Learn
to Make REAL Money in Real Estate Investment

Published by:

Vision Quest Media
27109 N 143 Pl
Scottsdale
AZ 85262

Order Information:

To order more copies of this book, please visit:

www.Creatingwealth101.com

Other Books:

Send In The Wolf

20 Insider Secrets to Building Real Wealth in the New Economy

Top 5 Rules For Investing in Real Estate In The New Economy

Other Services:

Turn-Key Property Acquisition
Public Speaking
Business Consulting
Real Estate Investment Training / Consulting

Contents

Part I

Acknowledgements

There is no such thing as a self-made man. I learned that lesson a long time ago. Many people seem to think they have made it all on their own, but the reality is that it takes help, lots of it. I have certainly come a long way in my life but I have no doubt that I would not be a fraction of what I am now without all those from throughout the years that lent their support.

My beautiful wife, Allison, who has been on this crazy roller coaster ride from the start. Being an entrepreneur is not for the faint of heart, and it sure is not easy. Being married to one is even harder. The sacrifices I made were, and are many, but it is her who pays the biggest price. I can't imagine how hard it is to put your full faith and trust in someone when you know most of their ideas are crazy, but that is what she does. Day in and day out, supporting me all the way. There is an old saying that behind every good man, is a good woman. In my case, a great woman.

My daughters Justine and Natalie. Where do I begin? The joy you have brought into my life cannot be put into words. I don't think you will ever know how happy you make me. I have never been so proud of something in my life. You keep me grounded. You make me laugh. You deal with my craziness as well as your mom, and

1

you always make sure I know that you love me. And in case you didn't know it, the two of you are my inspiration. You are the reason I do what I do. The greatness I see in you gives me hope in the future. I hope I make you proud. You are my heroes.

My Mom and Dad who have long since passed, but none-the-less, helped make me what I am today. They taught me kindness, compassion, work ethic, and most importantly, how to be a good person. My dad never complained about anything, at any time. He just did his work. He led by example, and that example was the greatest gift they could have given me.

My father-in-law, Harry Erb, one of the greatest entrepreneurs I have ever met. And my mother-in-law, Patty Erb, one of the strongest women I have ever met. I could never thank you enough for all you have done for me. You have always treated me like a son, and provided unwavering support through good times and bad. Thank you.

As entrepreneurs, we tend sometimes to stay inside our own head longer than we should. We sometimes shut out the outside world and take counsel only from ourselves. I have been guilty of this more than I would like to admit. On the occasions when I realize that I am not the one with all the answers, I have my "go to" guy. The Real Estate Rock Czar...Frank McKinney. For those who know Frank, I could probably just stop there. You get it. For those who don't know Frank, I would recommend that you try and make that happen. What do you say about someone who has reached a level of success that most can never even dream of, yet their humility and kindness are on the level of a Mother Theresa? This is one of the world's greatest entrepreneurs and he can have more than enough reasons to be "too busy" when you need advice, but he never is. He is always there for me, more than willing to share hard earned wisdom. As a mentor and a friend, I can only say that I am very lucky to have met Frank. The work he and his incredible wife, Nilsa, do through the Caring House Project Foundation, continues to be a daily inspiration for me, and all that know him. I owe a big debt of gratitude to you, my brother.

It always strikes me a strange when people mention those who have passed in their acknowledgments. It's not like they're going to read it right? However, I would be very remiss if I did not mention someone who had an impact on me that could only be called TREMENDOUS! Charlie "TREMENDOUS" Jones. Wow! I feel fairly safe in saying that the world has never seen, nor will again, that likes of Charlie. As was the case with Frank, Charlie was a very big success yet never acted like it. His sole purpose was to bring joy through his love of books, humor, and God. The first time I met Charlie, he invited me to come stay at his house. I thought I was special. I wasn't, he just made me feel that way. He made everyone feel that way. From his trademark bear hugs, to his booming voice, to his master sales skills of making you walk out of his book store with two dozen books, Charlie was a dynamo. Charlie always knew what to say when you needed to hear it, and he knew what lessons you needed to learn even when you didn't. My fondest memory of Charlie is when he made me go into a room at his house called the "Christmas Room" He and his wife Gloria kept this room decorated for Christmas all year so the underprivileged kids could come over any time they like. Charlie sensed that maybe I was a bit...uptight? He decided he was going to take me to the Christmas room and make me sing karaoke Christmas carols in celebration of "Jesus' birthday." I, of course, said,"No way! Not going to happen!" So much for that. Within minutes I was singing Christmas carols with Charlie, loud and proud. Just the two of us. He taught me that it's ok to laugh and it's ok to act like a kid. He also taught me that God was always there for me no matter how dark the night. They say when the student is ready, the teacher will appear. I'm glad I was ready, and I'm glad Charlie was the teacher.

Here is an interesting one for you. My friend and Attorney, Matt Nichols. Knowing the contentious relationship most have with Attorneys, that almost seems like an oxymoron. Matt, I am glad to say is an exception that rule. Not only is he a great Attorney, but a great friend as well. I can always count on him for a good laugh and good advice, both when needed. He is a credit to his profession.

One of the true "Good Guys" in the business is Andrew Waite. Andrew is the publisher of the great *Personal Real Estate Investor Magazine*. The investment real estate world has lots of black hats, but Andrew is leading the charge for the good guys. His publication is unsurpassed when it comes to getting the FACTS on the world of investment real estate. His tireless efforts to bring legitimacy back to the work of investment real estate have not gone unnoticed by me or countless others who are true believers in what this business can do for not only the bottom line of consumers, but the United States as well. I can always count on Andrew to be there as a friend and confidant when needed. I can also be assured of him never pulling any punches when it comes to something he feels I should know. Tough love, but much appreciated.

My sounding boards, Vince Parrucci, Mark Evans, Doug Doebler and Casey Reynolds. As I mentioned earlier, we entrepreneurs tend to stay in our own head too long at times. Having friends like Vince Mark, Doug and Casey to bounce things off of or just blow off some steam is something I never take for granted. The fact that they are "in the game" and "get me" is something that makes my life a lot easier. I'm not so sure what it does for them but hey, it works for me.

My old friend Kathy Svilar is owed a big thank you. Long before I reached the status of "big famous real estate guy", Kathy was the one who kept telling me that I was "really good" even when I didn't believe it myself. The great marketing and promotion work she did for me is without a doubt, a BIG part in my success. It is very difficult to put into words what Kathy did for my business but I think it is safe to say that without her on the team, our company would be nowhere near what it is today. Kathy holds the title of "one of the nicest" people in the world and she certainly proved that to me year in and year out. You go girl!

Picking up right where Kathy left off, Missy Wilson at Be Real Management. It is one thing to have a company who produces your radio shows and helps promote events. It is a COMPLETELY different thing to have someone who is a BIG cheerleader and believes in your product. Just like Kathy, Missy makes me look really good. And, she is a real estate investor! I am sure you know that we could not do this without you, but thank you VERY MUCH anyway. You are a Rock Star!

This book would not be possible if not for the help of my friend Rich Selby of Selby Marketing Associates. Rich has a fulfillment company in New York that supplies all of our CDs, DVDs, and anything else we need in order to help our business and our clients. Like Andrew Waite, Rich is one of the true good guys.

I also want to thank all of my clients past and current that have put their faith in me and allowed me to bring them in to the greatest business in the world. The case studies in this book are not just clients, but BIG inspirations. They took this business and they ran with it. They may be thanking me, but it is they, that make me look good. It is people like that, who are the spark that lights the economic engine in the Country.

A very special thank you to my ghost writer, Kathleen Birmingham. Kathleen showed me a sincere interest in this project from the very start. Being an entrepreneur herself, she understood the message I was trying to get across and managed to capture that message and still keep my voice in it. To say it has been easy working with her would be a very big understatement. She has been a pleasure through the entire process and I look forward to our next project.

Finally, I would like to thank all those out there who are looking for a better life. All those looking for a bit of hope, or a bit of light. They call you the dreamers. It is you people that make me very proud of the path I have chosen. The world, in the words of Rocky Balboa, "Ain't all sunshine and rainbows. It can be a "mean and nasty place that will chew you up and spit you out" And that is what happens to so many.

But what happens next, is what lights my fire. They get up. Against all odds, they get up, and fight again. That is what makes me stand up and applaud. The everyday people who understand, that life is not a dress rehearsal. It is show time and they are ready. Win, lose or draw, they are ready. I salute you. All of you. I hope this book makes things a bit easier for you. You're heading in the right direction....keep going.

Dedication

To:

My wife, Allison, the one that never fails me;

And my beautiful daughters Justine and Natalie, my pride and joy, thank you for making me want to be a better man.

Foreword

Willy Wonka, Robin Hood, Evel Knievel, Donald Trump, David Lee Roth, The Punisher, Mother Theresa... and Jim Toner. Each for their own reason, all are heroes, no, super-heroes to me. They shaped my life. I'll save the "why" for a future book of mine.

 For now, let's focus on why Jim Toner is a living super-hero to me and many.

First, allow me to welcome you to the most exciting, wild and potentially immensely profitable world if investment real estate. I love this world. It has been very good to me, now let's allow Jim to make is great for you too!

Before you read Jim's book, I want you to know that it passed an important litmus test of mine; can what you are holding in your hand move you from "inspiration" to "aspiration?" The answer is an unequivocal "YES!

Inspiration is great, but it wears off quickly. Aspiration, on the other hand, can alter your DNA, and stays with you for like. CONSUMER'S GUIDE TO INVESTMENT REAL ESTATE has the potential to do just that!

Please understand that this Consumers Guide is simply an OVERVIEW.

There is quite a bit to learn in the real estate business, too much to be crammed into the book you are holding.

Yet, CONSUMER'S GUIDE TO INVESTMENT REAL ESTATE will be very valuable in helping you understand what this business is really all about.

It will show you what you can accomplish if you follow a system that has worked for Jim and many others.

The wild economic ride we have been on the past few years has caused many to reevaluate their financial lives. One thing that many certainly understand is that there is no security in working for someone else.

You must make your OWN security.

Is it scary?

Yes.

Is it worth it?

An even bigger yes.

Remember this: When the opportunity for a big change or challenge presents itself you must risk, and the thought of risk is going to evoke fear. And that is a good thing.

So:

Change/Challenge = Risk = Fear = Good!

Besides being a super-hero, Jim is a friend, and also a board member of our Caring House Project Foundation (www/chpf.org).

Accomplishing the things I have done in the real estate and philanthropic world brings many people to my door step asking for endorsements. I am very cautious of who I offer endorsements to as many in this world are just "talkers" at best and snake oil salesmen at worst.

Jim is what I call a "DOER."

He says what he means and he gets things done. He closes the loop on initiatives he starts.

I remember years ago when Jim told me he was going to give away a debt free home to a returning veteran. That is no small feat, so I was not quite sure he would or could do it. Well, he did it. Not just once, but three times. That is a DOER, and that is someone you want to learn from.

The most important thing to know about Jim is that he is a REAL investor.

He has been in this business over 25 years and knows how things work in the real estate world.

He will share with you his successes and more importantly, he is willing to share his failures. Some of them VERY big failures. Why is sharing his failures so important? Because anyone who has been in this business for any length of time will meet with failure on some level. Anyone who does not admit it, and share what they could have done to avoid it is someone you want to steer clear of.

Jim understands that the consolation prize for failure is a lesson learned. Not a bad prize at all!

For my 25 years in real estate I can tell you that it has provided me with a life I could never have dreamed of.

Listen to, and then apply what Jim teaches you in this book. Who knows, maybe someday you will be added to that list of super real estate heroes!

~Frank McKinney

5-time bestselling author including:
Burst This! Frank McKinney's Bubble-Proof Real Estate Strategies
www.Burst-This.com

Introduction

No one wants to part with their hard-earned money.

And yet everyone would like to find a way to improve their quality of living, rebuild their retirement portfolios, and find a way to get out of the rat race and enjoy this journey through life.

Real estate investing is one of the only ways I know to build real wealth, wealth that you can see and touch. When you own real estate, you can walk on it, you can climb its stairs, open and close its doors.

The money we've all put into our retirement accounts is nothing but "funny money" until the day we withdraw it. It could be worth a whole lot of real money, or it might be worth less than the paper it is printed on.

Wall Street would like you to believe that investing in the stock market is the safest and surest way to wealth.

I'm here to tell you that they're wrong. The surest way to wealth is real estate.

It has always been real estate and it always will be real estate. People will always need a place to live, and when you're providing a good quality product for a good price, there will be a waiting list for your properties.

Real estate, in addition to being a tangible asset, provides other benefits such as tax advantages, instant equity, positive monthly cash flow and back end profits.

What real estate investing is **not**...is it is not a *"get rich quick"* scheme.

We prefer to see real estate investing as a *"get rich slow"* method to making your money work for you.

Make no mistake, this is a business. You will work it. Once you learn the tricks of the trade, you will decide how much time you want to spend on your investment real estate business. But, nothing ever happens with you doing something. I often tell people to look down at their own two feet. If those two feet aren't out there doing something, then your investment real estate business will also be doing nothing. Nothing happens without you doing something!

Once you learn the tricks of time-saving activities, you will see how this is a business that anyone can do. The only people who are "not qualified" to participate in investment real estate are those who have already taken themselves out of the game.

Is that you?

If so, give it another chance. Read about my start in investment real estate and then go on to the chapters with our Case Studies...these are ordinary everyday people who have chosen to get into investment real estate and have done very well. They will all tell you that there is nothing about them that makes them better suited to be a real estate investor than anyone else.

The biggest obstacle you will encounter is the one you create yourself. Of all the things I learned in this business, the first one was that I was the one getting in my way of being successful. Once I cleared that hurdle, I have never looked back.

Meet Jim Toner

Experts! Everywhere you turn, experts. No matter what it is you are looking for or into, you can no doubt find...an expert. Or you will at least find someone who "claims" to be.

Investment real estate is no different.

There is no shortage of people out there who will tell you how much they know and how much you don't know. However, should you be wise enough to follow their "expert" advice, you will be RICH!! Sounds good on paper.

In the real world...ahh...not so much.

So, am I a real estate investment expert? Probably not. I'm VERY good at what I do but sometimes I think the term "expert" means there is nothing more to learn. In the high stakes world of investment real estate, there is ALWAYS something to learn.

In my 25 years of "doing" this business it would be safe to say that I have learned a lot. Much of it, though very valuable, was very expensive.

My goal is to shortcut that for you so you can learn from my mistakes. Why not? I already paid for them.

This *How to Make Money in Real Estate* industry is a billion dollar a year enterprise. The unfortunate part is that much of it is dominated by what we call "The Black

Hats." Remember in the old Western movies the good guys wore the white hats and the bad guys wore the black?

Many of these "Black Hats" are VERY big names not only in the industry, but also with the general public. Unfortunately they use their name to get people into programs that more often than not leave the customer broke and not even able to complete a real estate transaction.

Later on in the book you will see a great interview I conducted with Andrew Waite, publisher of *Personal Real Estate Investor Magazine*, the industry's leading publication. Andrew will let you know what to look out for should you ever go to the seminars promoted by these "gurus."

How am I different? Simple, I *do* the business.

I *am* a real estate investor.

Yes, I am a speaker, author, and radio show host, but *primarily*, I am a real estate investor. As a matter of fact, everyone on my team is a real estate investor. That is the difference.

In my opinion, if you are not actively working this business, you have no right to teach it.

My goal with this book is to show you how anyone, with the proper mind set and knowledge, can succeed in the world of investment real estate.

Will you become the next Donald Trump? No, probably not.

Can you become a millionaire? Absolutely!

But what if that is not your goal. What if you are just looking to provide a better life for yourself and your family? Well, this is the best opportunity you will find. Making an extra $30,000 a year is not hard to do in this business. I understand that is not all the money in the world but that kind of money *will* make a difference in your life.

No doubt you will be surprised as I was to learn how easy it is to accumulate over a million dollars in real estate that will easily generate over $100,000 a year income for you.

I'm not sure about you, but in my opinion, it beats working.

It is not necessarily easy, but then again, what is? I will do my best to make it MUCH easier for you that it would be should you attempt this on your own.

By the way, DO NOT DO THAT! Don't try to figure this business out all by yourself. Be smart, and learn from my mistakes. Trust me, I have made them all.

I will show you the pitfalls to avoid and the things that you should aggressively pursue.

Finally, you will get to read some of our Case Studies. These are comprised of students who have gone through my real estate investing course and you will hear in their words exactly what they are doing with their knowledge and skill today.

All of these Case Studies have managed their deals long after the 2006 housing market crisis. As you read them, you will see that despite all the negative news in the media about the downfall of the housing market, there has never been a better time to get into real estate investing than now.

The person who decides to learn about real estate today and acts on that decision is going to be a very, very happy person about ten years from now. Why? Because they will be able to live the life they want to live, and they will only have to work a few hours a week to manage their properties and possibly add to their portfolio.

If this sounds like something that would interest you, read on. You will discover that there is real money to be made in real estate investing.

Entrepreneurs Don't Fit In

School was never for me. I'm not a genius. This isn't rocket science. I just learned the hard way not to do certain things. Now I want to share them with you.

I graduated from high school in 1980. The whole time I was growing up, I wasn't quite sure what I wanted to be. At the time, this really bothered me. I was surrounded by kids who intended to be doctors, lawyers, engineers, scientists, you name it. I could not settle on any single career that would be fulfilling to me.

What I discovered is that I'm an entrepreneur.

In all those years since high school, I've learned that entrepreneurs feel different from everyone else around them. They don't know where they should fit in. they can't understand what is happening. Now that I understand it, it makes perfect sense.

At the time, I just didn't understand why I felt so different and I never fit in.

I was not a very good student in high school...a C-student at best, barely graduating high school. Because scholastic studies never interested me, I didn't even consider going to college. So, what does someone do after high school if they're not going to college?

Work.

This was nothing new to me. I've always worked my whole life, having had jobs from the time I was sixteen. I knew what it was like to work hard, after all, I'm the son of a steel-worker. Dad always said, "Son, you work hard, keep your nose to the grindstone, and just keep moving forward. Always do the right thing."

And so I did that.

I got out of high school and I worked any number of jobs. I was a personal fitness trainer, I worked in a bank,

I put on roofs, I did bartending, I did everything. But, nothing was working out for me. I was doing what everybody said, which was the "age-old" plan of, "Get a good job, work real hard, and just keep your nose to the grindstone."

I did that, but it didn't work for me. I was falling further and further behind and I could not understand what the problem was.

One day, I was sitting in my tiny one-bedroom apartment in a really bad section of Pittsburgh, Pennsylvania. Some of my buddies were meeting at the bar to get a sandwich and some beer and I planned on joining them.

My only problem was, I didn't have any money in my wallet. I did have a glass jar that I would put my spare change into, so I took that over to the plastic outdoor table that served as my dining room table and took my seat in the matching green chair.

Hey, my furniture was plastic patio furniture, but at least they all matched in color.

I poured the contents of the jar onto the table and started separating the coins. Not as many quarters as I would have liked. I could just see me handing over fistfuls of coins tonight in exchange for a beer and a burger. I'd certainly get a ton of razzing before we launched into our favorite topic, "How Bad Life Is."

What was I doing with my life? Where had I gone wrong? I considered myself to be a good guy, working hard at two jobs. Why wasn't the plan, "Get a good job, work real hard, and keep your nose to the grindstone," working for me?

There was a serious flaw in my system, and I just couldn't see it.

I looked around my dismal little apartment and felt a flash of fear run straight through my body.

Was this all there was?

Was life really not going to get any better?

I'd done everything I'd ever been told about being successful, but I just kept falling further and further behind.

My eyes stopped looking around having caught sight of something that would change my life. I stared at a book lying on the floor. Someone had given it to me, a copy of Napoleon Hill's *Think and Grow Rich.*

I barely read books in high school, and I have to admit, until that moment I hadn't picked up a book since then.

I don't know, maybe I was desperate that night. Maybe I was intrigued by the idea of just thinking about getting rich and having it happen. Seriously, I just don't know what prompted my next action, but I picked that book off the floor and started reading.

That one act changed my life forever.

The book you never read can't help you. That book had been lying on the floor of my apartment for as long as I'd been there. I just didn't pay any attention to it. I'd get up every morning, go to work, and hope to have enough money to meet the guys at the bar in the evening.

I must have walked past that book a thousand times.

That night, I read that book and my eyes were finally opened. I finally understood why I never felt "normal" around everyone in high school. The entrepreneurial spirit was buried deep inside of me and I had to realize it before it could reveal itself to me.

For most of my life, my goal was always to make a lot of money; I just didn't know how to do it. Frankly, I really didn't even care how I made the money. I just wanted to make money. Anytime anyone asked me how I intended to do it, I was pretty vague about what I wanted to do. What I did know was that I had to get out of this seriously deep rut I found myself in.

But how could I do that?

I'd never had any specific plans on getting into real estate investing. Admittedly, I was always intrigued by the "rags to riches" stories that were portrayed on those infomercials about how these ordinary people got rich. I remember thinking, "Wow! That would be really cool!"

So, yes, I'd been intrigued by the real estate infomercials, but I immediately disqualified myself from using these as the vehicle to my new life of wealth. I established barriers faster than Usain Bolt can run the 100 meter dash. I didn't know how to do contracting work. I didn't know how to do accounting. I knew nothing about real estate. I had no money and my credit score was so low that any bank would have laughed at me if I had tried to get a loan.

Real estate investing might work for some people. But not for me.

I just blew the idea off.

And I kept blowing it off until the night I read *Think and Grow Rich.* All of a sudden I understood the concept called the Mastermind Technique or the Mastermind Principle. This is where you surround yourself with talented people who are working on your behalf; you don't have to be an expert in anything.

You just surround yourself by talented experts.

It was like a light bulb went off. "Wow! I don't have to know how to do this! I can plug in the people who do!" This revelation gave me some confidence.

The next logical step was to invest in one of those programs I kept seeing on television, a "Get Rich Real Estate" course. I could hardly wait for the course to come. I listened to every single recording in that set probably two dozen times. I did everything they recommended, but I wasn't making any money.

At the time, what I didn't understand was that there was good information in that course, but it was all *general* information.

I'm here to tell you that general information just doesn't cut it in this business.

One day, I was sitting at my green plastic table reading the newspaper, because the course told me to read the newspaper and look for things. I didn't know what it was I was supposed to be looking for, but every day I would obediently open the newspaper and *look*.

Then one day I saw an ad that said, "I buy houses."

Aha! This guy must be a real estate investor. This was another light bulb moment for me. I'd been doing everything my course had told me to do and I wasn't making money. I had read about real estate investing, I'd seen the infomercials on TV, but I didn't actually know anyone who did real estate investing for a living.

This is what I needed! I needed to talk to an expert in the field. Once I talked to him I was sure that I would know that this path was the one for me.

Making that call took guts, I can tell you. The phone rang and he actually answered, "Hello?"

"Uh, hi...I saw your ad in the paper..."

"Do you have a house for sale?"

"No." Silence. I wasn't quite sure how to ask, so I just blurted it out, "Are you an investor?"

He replied, "Yes, I am."

"Great! I'm looking for some help and I wonder if I can get some advice from you."

"Kid, I'm not interested in handing out advice." The guy was blowing me off!

This was my first introduction into the world of real estate investing. The old-timers out there, the ones who are really making money, are not going to tell you anything.

I didn't know this at the time, so even though I was taken aback, I wasn't above begging, "Please! I am really looking to get into the business. If I could just get ten minutes of your time..."

I finally convinced this guy to meet me. We met at a coffee shop in Pittsburgh. I found out later he was working out of his basement. He looked me in the eye and said, "So, you want to be a real estate investor?"

"Yeah! I really do!"

"Do you know anything at all about real estate investing?"

"No. I know absolutely nothing."

"So you have any money?"

OK, this felt like a sucker punch. "No."

He looked at me for a minute like I was some kind of bug under a microscope. Apparently he thought he saw an opportunity to make a buck off of me. "Well, for me to teach you what I know, it's going to cost you $2,500 and half the profit from the first few deals we do."

He might just as well have said $25,000. I didn't have twenty-five dollars, let alone twenty-five hundred. My discouragement must have shown on my face, because right then he was the one encouraging me, "Don't worry...we'll make money."

I wasn't sure what I expected from that meeting, but I do remember leaving feeling completely dejected. Then I fell into the trap that most people who look at real estate investing and then immediately come up with reasons why it won't work.

All the way back to my lonely and cramped apartment I kept thinking of all these horror stories of why it wouldn't work, and all the horrible things that would happen to me if I tried and failed.

But, then there was a part of me, deep down inside that asked a question that I genuinely wanted to answer, "What if it *did* work?"

That made me reevaluate everything. What if it was a scam and I lost money, would I be completely destroyed?

No.

It would hurt, but I wouldn't be destroyed. Heck, I was already living a "destroyed" life in my opinion. There was really only one way to go from my present state in life, and that was up.

So, what if it were real? What if it really worked?

If it really worked my life would never be the same again. That was a risk I was willing to take.

I decided to take the leap.

One of the real estate tapes I had been listening to said, "Real estate is a calculated risk." So, I figured it was time for me to take that calculated risk.

Dialing that investor's number again made me sick with fear and giddy with anticipation all at the same time. When he answered the phone I said, "I'm in."

That's it. I made the decision and nothing was going to stop me.

My next move was to figure out how to put the money together. And trust me, that was an obstacle, but one I was determined to overcome.

The only possession I had at the time was a handmade Ovation acoustic guitar. I sold it and got $600 for that custom guitar. I also had an amp that I sold with it, so between the guitar and the amp, my buyer was happy to part with his money.

For the rest of my fee, I went to American General Finance and they surprised me by agreeing to loan me the rest of the money for 18% interest. I figured I might just as well figure out how to do this now, and learning costs money.

I paid the guy the money and we got started.

My Real Estate Investing Education

We did a few deals, and sure enough, I made my money back.

What was *really* ironic is that I actually knew more than my mentor did as far as technique. This was because I'd been buying and studying all those tapes and courses. The key was I didn't know how to *apply* the information.

The first thing we did was go out and do a wholesale deal. This is where we're not selling a property; we're selling the contract to the property. We get a property under contract and then sell it for a mark-up.

Within a few deals I was able to pay off the loan from the bank, plus I had $5,000 in the bank.

Right there was the major mental shift.

The money was great, but the payoff is what happened mentally. Now, I had gone from someone who saw it, heard about it, talked about it to somebody who *did* it.

Paying off my credit cards was an unbelievable relief to me. I was able to get myself a stereo system, pay my rent in advance, and I still had money left over.

The words that had been pounded into me, "Work hard, go to school, get a job, keep your nose to the grindstone," continued to whirl around in my head. But, what I began to wonder is, "Maybe there is a flaw in that plan. Maybe it's not about working harder and keeping my nose to the grindstone. Maybe it's about working smarter."

Maybe it's about looking at things from a different perspective.

I was able to do those first deals with no money, and no credit, yet I was making more money than I made in half a year at my job. I'd been making about $10,000 a year at my job, but it wasn't doing the trick. It took a big chunk of change to get me out of debt.

You can't nickel and dime your way out of debt.

Neither can you nickel and dime your way into wealth.

You need something that can generate a big hit, and I figured out very quickly for me that it was real estate.

We've all considered other ways of developing income.

- Franchise – that's nothing but another J.O.B.
- Invest in the stock market. How's your 401k doing?
- Get a Second Job? I was already putting in enough hours with my first job.

Real estate was it for me!

I knew I was jumping in and there was no turning back.

Before I became successful in doing deals with my first mentor, I had disqualified myself from becoming a real estate investor. I felt that because I didn't go to college I wasn't educated enough to be successful.

I was also afraid that if I got into real estate investing I would have to become a contractor and do all the things I've done in past jobs. I didn't want to do those things before, and I sure didn't want to do them now.

Yet, those real estate investing infomercials on late night TV kept intriguing me. They certainly showed the lifestyle I wanted. They showed checks for $20,000 and that was two years' salary for me at the time.

I wanted to believe that real estate investing would work the way they said it would.

Once I got into it, I found out it did! But what they don't tell you is that real estate investing is a business and you have to work it like a business.

It is **not** a get rich quick scheme.

But, I do like to call it a "Get Rich Quicker" Plan!

With real estate, I know where my money is. I can see it, I can touch it, and it's really there. When you buy a property, your money is in that property. Everyone needs a place to live, *that's* not a fad! Everyone has to have a roof over their heads.

My experience with my first mentor got me over the fear and obstacles I had erected. All the information I had learned from the tapes and books turned me into an obsessive learner. I went from never opening a book in high school to devouring everything I could get my hands on in terms of real estate, business, and entrepreneurism.

Once the fear was gone, there was no stopping me.

Getting Started On My Own

The first deal I did by myself was a house just down the street from my new apartment. I kept driving by this foreclosed property thinking, "This is a really nice neighborhood. I wonder what they want for that property." I figured it was in the neighborhood of $80,000.

I called the number on the sign and found out that it was being sold for $30,000 because it needed a lot of work.

We went to see the property and while it needed some work, it wasn't anything insurmountable. The problem I had was I didn't have $30,000 yet.

Here's one of the lessons I learned, one of the tough lessons that most people don't know...I didn't know that foreclosures had to be purchased cash.

You can't get a mortgage on a foreclosure.

I had to come up with $30,000 in cash.

For a moment I allowed the reality of that statement to stop me. I didn't have thirty grand. But I liked that house. I did my numbers, got estimates on rehabbing and I knew there was a chance to make some good money. The house could sell for $80,000 once it was fixed up.

Basically, I found five investors.

This is another thing that keeps people from getting into estate investing, when they can't get a loan from the banks they stop right there.

I couldn't get a loan from the bank at that time either. But I didn't let it stop me. I saw the profit at the end and I just had to get at that profit. By finding private investors, I came up with the money I needed for that property.

And I got ripped off all along the way on that deal.

Yes. You read that right...I got ripped off by just about everyone on that first solo deal. The real estate agent, the contractors, landscaper, the attorney who did the closing all ripped me off. I should have made over $30,000 on that deal and I ended up clearing $17,000.

When I realized I'd been taken advantage of by all these so-called professionals, I was pretty angry.

And yet, I still made more money in a single deal than I'd made in my life!

Better yet, this time, I had done it on my own.

I was able to pay everybody back. Again I had the realization that I had made so many mistakes on this particular deal yet I still came out ahead.

How many businesses can you go into, make all the mistakes you possibly can and still make money?

Later I discovered I was pretty lucky not to have lost my shirt. This is why I don't want you to do what I did. Learn from my mistakes!

The end of Investment Real Estate as you knows it?

In the first edition of this book, back in 2012, during the recession, I wanted to make a point that becoming a successful real estate investor, was all about attitude and strategy and not economy. In the midst's of the biggest economic crash since the Great Depression, when the entire world was afraid to even breathe, I decided to take a handful of people, show them a few simple strategies, gave them a sounding board, and turned them loose into the market place.

You can read the results for yourself, but they were outstanding. By the way, during this time it was very interesting that all the "Guru's" who were so adept at "making millions" and "making YOU millions" had disappeared. Hmmm...I wonder why?

Now, we find ourselves in 2016 and depending on which economic "expert" you are listening to, and I use that term very loosely, we are either in a bit of a recovery, or we are headed for another recession.

What we do know however is that the "Guru's" are back and back in full force. You cannot find a City in the U.S that is not being flooded with "get rich seminars" by Rock Star investors. Their claim to fame is that maybe you have seen them on a TV. Infomercial, or you have heard their ads on the radio 10,000 times or any number of reasons as to why they are the answer to your financial prayers and all you need to do is show up at the FREE seminar to find out how.

And this is the end of investment real estate, as we know it my friends. I will talk in a later chapter about what goes on at these seminars, but for now, what I will tell you that at best, they may motivate some to get into the game. At worst, people get fleeced for tens of thousands of dollars and never even get a deal.

Suddenly, there are "new and improved" strategies that will finally get you over the hump and on the road to riches.

Let me turn you on to a little secret about real estate investment. Ready? It's the people business. It's a problem solving business. It's a business just like any other businesses that contains a few core principles that if followed correctly, really can dramatically turn around your financial life. But here is the big danger...it IS a business and the second you forget that, look out

And this is what is so concerning to me. The "new" things being taught or I should I say, sold, to you are planting seeds that will most likely cause you to FORGET, that you are going into a business.

You get pushed, willingly, into the "Millionaire Lifestyle" mindset and tell yourself, "go big or go home" Just my opinion but, it seems to me that the bigger many people get, the dumber they get. Just saying.

So much of what is going on out there truly is the blind leading the blind. These "guru's" if you shined the light on them, would run for cover because you will see what is REALLY going on in their world and they don't want that.

The truth about this biz, and I have been in it for over 27 years, is this. You don't need to be the next Donald Trump. You don't need to own 200 properties. You don't need the latest greatest strategies, and websites and social media platforms etc.

What you need are the strategies discussed in this book, a great attitude, team or mentor and a real plan. Look, the great thing about this business is that just 12 little properties can make you a millionaire.

You know the old timers' you see walking the neighborhoods...the ones that look like bums but they have 50K in cash in their pocket and own the neighborhood? How do you think they did it? Small deals, one at a time...the people business.

Later on I will also show you how to get into what I think everyone should be into and that is HANDS OFF INVESTING. Being a landlord stinks. The money is GREAT, but the other stuff, not so much. So, can you have your cake and eat it too? Sure can and I think your going to LOVE this cake.

I think this is the greatest business ever created, why? Because everyone needs a place to live. Our job is to give it to them and to use the KISS method.

Keep It Simple Stupid.

Ready?

Real Estate In Today's World

Why are you here?

Why are you reading this book?

You don't have to hide. We all know…you want to know if you have what it takes to make money in the real estate investing business. You've seen the infomercials, read the same "rags to riches" stories that inspired me and now you want to know if you have what it takes.

I'm glad you're here. Unless you're absolutely determined to do exactly the opposite of what you learn in this book, you're bound to know a whole lot more than when you started.

Will you learn everything you need to know?

No.

You wanted an honest answer, didn't you? And that honest answer is truly, "No!" I've been in the real estate investing business for 25 years and I'm still learning, so you can't possibly learn everything there is to know in one single book.

What you will learn is how to spot potential scams that are designed to only separate you from your hard-earned cash. You'll also learn that not all "bargains" are truly bargains. Ultimately, however, I want you to develop the courage to act on your dream of getting wealthy the slow way.

Building wealth in real estate takes time. Sure, some of the case studies will show you how they might have made many thousands of dollars in a single deal. That's pretty darn exciting! But, one windfall success does not make a successful real estate investor. You'll know you're successful when you can repeat your success over and over and over.

So, read on. You'll learn a lot about this industry and know that the biggest thing that is keeping you from being successful is yourself.

Once you get over that, the sky's the limit.

ROI in Real Estate is the Fast Track to Millions

It used to be that real estate investing belonged only to the rich and famous, or at least the very rich. Many of the very wealthy early Americans earned their money in real estate. Statistics have demonstrated that over 76% of American millionaires have earned their wealth through real estate.

Now you can step into that same arena and begin improving your bottom line with passive income.

One of the most powerful wealth builders ever created is leverage. By using leverage correctly you can literally control millions of dollars' worth of real estate with very little out of your own pocket.

Leverage allows you to make money off of the bank's money, as opposed to a stock where you can only make money off of what you put in.

For instance, if you buy a home for $100,000 and put $20,000 down, the bank finances the other 80%. But when it sells, instead of you making money off just your 20%, you make money off the entire investment. This is the power of leverage and why, when used correctly, it is a rapid wealth builder.

What's Your Retirement Plan?

You know where I'm going with this, don't you?

Yes, I'm going to ask you how your 401k is doing. Hey, I understand...I've talked to hundreds of people in my classes who have shared with me their fear that they will never be able to retire because their retirement funds have dwindled so much and they are afraid they will never recover.

There's a good reason for this fear.

I often ask the people who take my seminars, "Who in this room has a retirement plan?" Hands go up.

Then I get more specific. "Who in this room knows exactly when they're going to retire, at what age?"

Only a couple hands go up.

And then I ask the one no one wants me to ask, "How much money will you need and how are you going to get it?

No one's hand goes up because no one really knows.

One of the certainties in life is that you're going to retire. But do you know how you're going to do it? We used to be able to say, "I work for a good company, I have a secure pension." That's not the case anymore.

A few folks will say, "Well, I have Social Security."

I call that "So-So" Security. Will it be there? Even if it is, will that provide you with the same type of lifestyle you're living now?

I'm going to really scare you now. In order to retire, you might like to have $100,000 a year. Most people think that they can live on this.

That sounds like a lot of money.

But just how much will that $100,000 be in fifteen years? It's not going to be a whole lot of money.

Let's look at this scenario...let's say our investments are doing really well and we're getting 5% on our money. Treasury Bills are at about 2%. Maybe people will have money in a bank account, but even with interest, they're losing money because of inflation.

If you're getting 5% on your money and it is generating $100,000 in income, you need two million dollars.

$2,000,000.00

Most people think, "If I had two million dollars, I'd retire right now."

That's not such a good idea. Let's say you retire at 50, you're broke at 70. People are living into their 80s now. It isn't easy to save two million dollars.

But, with twelve single-family homes, just twelve...not two hundred...not twelve apartment buildings you can get your two million dollars in assets generating over $100,000 a year in income.

Twelve properties **owned free and clear** valued at only $167,000 each are worth over two million dollars. If those properties were rented for only $700 a month each, that is over $100,000 a year in income.

That's your retirement plan!

In addition to a better ROI, investing in real estate gives you additional tax benefits that you probably never even considered. Some of my students have formed companies that actually pay them for their time.

For example, if you were to be rehabbing a house and you wanted to do some of the tile work yourself (not my best recommendation, but you'll consider this so I'll cover it).

You will get money for doing that work...maybe only about twenty bucks an hour, but if that suits you, then you can do it.

Don't look to this book to give you any tax or accounting advice, however. You need to see your CPA (Certified Public Accountant) or your Attorney for advice in these areas.

What I want to do, however, is to open your eyes to the possibilities of being your own boss. Most of my students have been tied to Corporate America for so long that they aren't sure what an entrepreneur even does.

Until my next book on entrepreneurs comes out, suffice it to say that you will surround yourself with people who are expert at things you are not. You don't have to be an expert at everything. Find people who are experts at things and hang out with them.

Riches in Your Backyard and Beyond

I'm going to quote something you've all heard, "The other man's grass is always greener."

And it might seem like it in the real estate market. But you can actually become wealthy by investing in your own back yard as long as you take the time to understand the real estate investing environment of your back yard.

I've been investing in Pittsburgh, Pennsylvania for most of my investing career because despite the downturn in the market, Pittsburgh has managed to hold its own in the housing bubble.

People need a place to live.

They don't want to live on the street! They want comfortable and affordable housing. That's the kind of thing that I provide as a real estate investor. I'm not a slumlord. I make sure my houses and rental properties are rehabbed and very comfortable. I have a long list of people who want to rent one of my properties.

When you establish a reputation like that, the only place for you to go is up!

Another option is investing nationally.

Smart investors go where the money is. With today's advances in real estate investing, you have the opportunity to invest in the top markets in the country even if you don't live there. You also can have someone facilitate the entire process for you.

Learn from Experts not Naysayers

Take advice from people who are walking the walk. I've been in real estate investing for over 25 years, and there isn't much I don't know about this business.

Listen to the experts. Choose an experienced mentor.

Do not take advice from people who have never done this business. This includes some of the self-proclaimed "gurus" out there who might think they know a lot about real estate investing, but don't do it. Sadly, there are a few really big names out there who do just that, claim to be experts, but have never completed a real estate investment deal in their life.

Ask questions and get solid answers.

Also, try not to listen to concerned friends and family members who will try to talk you out of becoming a real estate investor just because they have heard horror stories.

It doesn't pay to listen to someone who has never set foot in the real estate investing arena. Sure, there are people who had made mistakes in real estate investing, but have they followed all the correct advice they've been given? Or, have they just tried to crack the market thinking they have enough of the answers, but failed to see a pitfall that cost them a lot of money?

This advice applies not just to real estate investing, but to most things in life.

Take your advice from experts...the people who are doing what you want to do.

There may be people around you who care about you and are concerned about you. But they know nothing about what you're trying to do.

It is ***their*** fear that can get in the way.

Don't let their fear stop you from living your life.

Lose Your FEAR

What is fear?

> **F**alse
>
> **E**vidence
>
> **A**ppearing
>
> **R**eal

This is how I have defined fear, both for myself and for my students. You will hear quite a bit about fear in the Case Studies section of this book where my students talk about their experiences with FEAR.

All fear does is inhibit your progress. Educate yourself. When you know what you're facing, your fears will vanish. Before I really got started, I allowed fear to hold me back. I had educated myself to death about real estate investing, but because I hadn't seen it done, I was afraid of that big unknown.

Fear is the big monster in the closet we hope won't get us. It's not real, but we believe it is.

Once you know the real answers to your questions you will no longer be stumbling around in the dark, guessing and hoping that you made the right decisions.

Real estate investing can be risky business, but the risk is manageable. By getting started under the guidance of a coach or mentor, you are mitigating a lot of that risk. When I first started, I was so afraid to just jump into real estate investing that I kept procrastinating. Once I found a mentor, I discovered that I actually knew more than he did, but he didn't have the fear I did.

What I had to get over was my fear.

Once I banished fear, my life changed forever.

What Does Today's Real Estate Investor Look Like?

Sorry, I'm not going to hold up a mirror and say, "Hey, today's real estate investor looks just like you!"

Wait!

Maybe I should!

There is no such thing as a "typical" real estate investor. If you have the right mindset and determination, you can be a real estate investor. Trust me, I almost made a mistake one time during my interview process. I was interviewing a guy who wanted to be part of my mentoring program and he just didn't have the outward appearance of a "go-getter" and I was about ready to say that I wasn't comfortable taking his money.

Then, I thought to ask him what he did for a living...it turns out that this guy had been a door-to-door salesman for over ten years!!! Anyone in that industry knows that door-to-door sales is about the hardest job in the world. If this guy could be successful for that long in that job, he would surely be successful as a real estate investor.

And sure enough, he did absolutely great. I learned the hard way that you can't judge how well someone is going to do by how they look. The last I heard, this door-to-door salesman had eleven or twelve properties in his portfolio.

One thing I have learned, however, is that there is one type of person who doesn't do quite as well at real estate investing as most others, and that is the overly analytical person. In my experience, engineers find it hard to get into real estate investing because they need to analyze everything.

And even when they have analyzed everything, then they want to wait and thing about things.

In this business, you've got to be able to pull the trigger. When you have a deal where you can make $20,000 to $25,000, it's not going to sit there for three weeks while you think about it!

There's a phrase I use with my students. "Math doesn't lie. Period. Here are the numbers." Once you have the numbers on a deal and you know the numbers, you either do it or you don't. There is no thinking about it.

You have to be someone who can take action and pull the trigger.

I've turned away more engineers from my courses than anyone else and they're stunned when I won't take their money. I just know that they aren't going to succeed because they will not be able to act on a deal fast enough.

Now, before all you engineers out there get offended, I've had some engineers as students and they've done an incredible job with their real estate investing business. One of the case studies in this book is about an engineer who turned to real estate investing to make a difference in his life. You know yourself better than anyone. If you find it difficult to make a decision, to act on something, even when it might be a really good deal for you, this just might not be the business for you.

You're NOT Buying a House for You

Probably the biggest hurdle most new real estate investors experience is learning that they are not buying a home for themselves or their family.

Why is this important?

Think about it. When you go looking at houses you want to live in, to create a home for your family, you're really looking for a property that is move-in ready. You're not looking to do a lot of renovation before you install your family there. You might be relocating (which is pretty darn stressful, and a less than perfect house does not make for marital bliss), so you want a "home sweet home" pretty fast.

When you're investing in real estate, you know that the number one rule is you make your money on the purchase. This means you're looking for houses that pretty much no one else really wants to touch. You're going to hear over and over again how my students want "the rougher the better" type of properties.

As a real estate investor, when your Realtor says, "You don't want to look at that house, the foundation's crumbling, or the roof's leaking, or the copper pipe has been pulled from the walls."

I have two pieces of advice:

- #1: Fire that Realtor. They aren't listening to what you want.
- #2: Yes, you DO want to look at that house if the other numbers are adding up.

One of my students says, "I smell money," when he sees things like a tarp over the roof of a foreclosed house. He's often right...the houses that other people won't touch are often pure gold, but we'll get into more of that later.

Get a Mentor!

You need a mentor. Please trust me on this. At least in the beginning, get yourself a mentor.

If it isn't me, please get someone who will be there to guide you through the puzzles and traps that are bound to confront you. I got a mentor, and even though I discovered pretty quickly that I knew more than he did, his guidance gave me the courage and confidence I needed.

After you've done a few deals with a mentor, you're probably going to be ready and totally capable of running your own real estate investing business. The nice thing about having a mentor is that you can call him/her up and bounce ideas back and forth. An experienced mentor can save you countless hours and probably thousands of dollars on a deal that isn't quite right.

Remember too, mistakes in this business can put you out of business.

Build a Circle of Experts

Unless you've been into investment real estate before, you'll need to build what I call your Circle of Experts. These are the people you will lean on, count on as you follow this journey.

You want people you can trust, so don't just pick out some guy who has the biggest ad in the Yellow Pages. (I know, that is an old enough analogy that I'm really dating myself.) But, that's exactly what I did when I was looking for an attorney.

I picked the guy who had the biggest ad in the phone book.

I figured, "He has a big ad, he must be a good guy." On the contrary, this guy knew how to spot an inexperienced sucker and soaked me for many thousands of dollars before I wised up.

Instead, talk to people. Ask who they use and why they like working with certain individuals. Talk to a lot of people and get as many references as you can.

Remember, this is *your* money we're talking about here. You've worked hard for it, so don't throw it down the drain just because you're afraid of offending someone with your questions.

If you're too afraid to check someone's references, you probably shouldn't be in this business.

You'll need a real estate agent who understands the mindset of the investor. Not an agent who only knows how to deal with a retail client.

When you get into refurbing or rehabbing, you'll want an excellent general contractor. You might want two or three after you get going because you may have enough work for that many. Not all general contractors are created equal, so plan on going through quite a few of them until you find the perfect fit.

Once you find the perfect fit, don't ever let them go.

You'll need a few other people in your circle of experts, perhaps a property manager if you aren't going to be handling tenants yourself.

Surround yourself with people who know more about their job than you do. Just make sure you know that they're treating you fairly.

If it works well for both of you, that's the beginning of a very long relationship.

Know How to Evaluate the Deal

You will hear, "The numbers don't lie," many times throughout this book. And they don't.

When you know how to evaluate a potential deal, it takes all the emotion out of making a real estate investing decision.

Beginning real estate investors often don't know how to evaluate a deal. They think they are making a good deal, or they allow themselves to be convinced that they're getting a good deal.

Even worse, because their friends and neighbors know that they're getting into real estate investing, they try to sell their properties to this beginning real estate investor, promising that it's a great deal.

Usually, it isn't. And that is how experience and the proper training will save your bacon.

You're becoming a real estate investor in order to make money. You're **not** becoming a real estate investor to buy non-bargains from friends and family.

By learning to evaluate a property opportunity, it takes all the emotion out of it. If the numbers say it is a good deal, it's a good deal. If the numbers say it is not a good deal, then you must walk away if you intend to keep making money in this business.

Trust me, my friend. The numbers *don't* lie.

Money, Money, Money

The days of banks providing loans to anyone with a pulse are long gone. In order to borrow money from a bank, you need to have good credit and a way to pay back the money before you will ever be considered for a loan.

Does this mean that you will never qualify for a loan? Does it mean you can't get into real estate investing? Not if you can find other ways to fund your new business.

Yes, you do need money for most aspects of real estate investing. There are a few ways to conduct deals, such as wholesaling, but for the most part, you need to fund your business. There are quite a few ways to find the necessary money to run your real estate investing business.

Personal Wealth

Obviously the first place to look is at your own personal wealth, or your own net worth. If you use some financial software that keeps track of your finances, then running a Net Worth report will give you a rough idea within seconds.

The way to calculate your net worth is to make a listing of all your current assets, cash, checking and savings accounts. Do you have any long-term assets such as CDs, life insurance that has cash value, stocks, bonds, existing real estate, cars, trucks, RVs, IRAs, etc.?

Once you've tallied up all your assets, it's time to look at your liabilities, or what you owe to someone else. These include bills, mortgages, loans, and taxes.

Subtract your liabilities from your assets and that is a rough number for your net worth. Obviously, this is pretty simplified, but you need to have an idea of what you're worth. Your CPA or accountant can also help you with this, or you can download forms from the internet to help you identify all your assets and liabilities.

Equity

If you already own a home, you might want to see how much equity you have in your home now. That equity can then be used as a down payment for a piece of property. Just make sure you know your numbers. You don't want to risk your own home on a dicey investment. But, as long as you're wise about how you do this, home equity is an excellent source of cash.

Family/Friends (Developing Investors)

After working with my original mentor, I realized that I knew about as much as he did, if not more. What he managed to do was to get me over my fear of taking action. I made some money, I learned what I needed to learn and I was able to move on and start investing on my own. I moved to a new apartment in a better part of town and as I was driving around I noticed a foreclosed property for sale. I figured they would want about $80,000 for the property, but I checked into it anyway.

I called the number on the sign, "How much do they want for this house?"

"Well, it needs a lot of work so they're asking $30,000."

I asked to see the property and once inside I could see that it needed to be refurbished, but it wasn't anything insurmountable. But with this one, I learned a big lesson. I didn't know that foreclosures had to be purchased with cash...I couldn't get a mortgage on it.

I didn't have $30,000.

And yet, I liked the house. When I worked the numbers after getting estimates on rehabbing, I knew there was a good chance of making some good money on this house. If I could get the house for $30,000 and then put $20,000 into the rehab, I could sell it for $80,000 and make more money than I would typically make in two years.

I begged, borrowed, and stole...ok, not really, but you get the picture. I basically found five investors to back me.

So many people who want to get into this business stop because they can't get a loan from a bank. That stops them in their tracks. I couldn't get a loan from a bank yet. My credit was better, but I wasn't an ideal candidate for them yet.

But I didn't let that stop me. I saw profit in that opportunity, so I found private investors among my friends and family and borrowed all the money I needed.

You're Going to Get Ripped Off

Unless you really know what you're doing, you're going to have people rip you off. It's part of the business.

On this deal, I got ripped off by everyone involved in the transaction. The real estate agent, the contractors, the landscaper, the attorney who did the closing. I should have made over $30,000 on that deal, but in the end I only cleared $17,000.

I hired some contractors, and while I wasn't a contractor, I had been a laborer, so I knew what had to be done. I saw their ad in the paper and I hired them to work for me by the hour. I didn't know it at the time, but you don't pay contractors this way. For four days I paid these guys at the end of every day, even though when I would look around it didn't look as though much was getting done. They kept telling me there was a lot of preparation that had to be done before I'd see any progress.

They fleeced me for over $500 before I got wise to them. I learned then that you don't ever pay a contractor by the hour.

My roofing contractor gave me a bid for $3,000 to repair part of a flat roof that was leaking. After they were done, it still leaked. I had to have it redone by another contractor who told me it shouldn't have cost more than $1,600.

By this time, you should be getting the picture...I believed the ads these guys were putting in the paper.

I didn't check their references.

Check references...on EVERYONE!

At the time, I had no idea how to handle contractors. Now, I've got everything figured out down to the last nail and nickel. One of the things we teach our clients is how to become experts at dealing with contractors, the questions to ask, the contracts to use with them, and how they should perform for you.

Then, in the same deal, the real estate was talking about the offer with another agent, working together to improve the commission for both of them. This kind of thing happens quite often. In fact, I got my real estate license when I finally just got sick and tired of dealing with incompetent real estate agents. For the most part, they don't understand what an investor is looking for. They're just used to being a tour-guide, "Here's the kitchen, here's the master bedroom." I don't need a real estate to tell me that, I need them to find the properties for me.

It was a slightly disillusioning time for me because I held Realtors in pretty high esteem when I first started in this industry. I thought they would be part of my team. But just like everyone else, you can't just pick someone and have them work out. You have to check them out, check their references, check their past clients/customers.

Then the last one to take advantage of my ignorance was my attorney. He charged me thousands of dollars to do my closings and I found out later that his fees should only be about $150 to $200 for what I needed him to do. He was also putting costs on me that should have been on his end.

This is the trap that people walk into. I thought that professionals in the industry would be honest and forthright, my contractors, my Realtors, and my attorney all ripped me off.

Interestingly enough, while I was upset at being ripped off, I still came out ahead. I had more money on this deal where I had been ripped off than I had ever made in my life! For me, these were incredibly valuable lessons.

Make Your Money When You Purchase

The thing is, I still made money on this purchase because I had run the numbers. Yes, I would have made a lot more money if I hadn't been scammed at every turn, but the point is, I still walked away with a lot of money.

I played into Rule Number One in real estate: you make your money when you buy, not when you sell.

I was able to buy this piece of property low enough that even though I got ripped off all along the way, I still walked away with a lot of money.

Always, always, always check your numbers.

Don't get caught up in the emotion of things. Don't try to do a friend a favor. Don't listen to your real estate agent if they aren't a specialist in investment property.

You do the math.

If the numbers are right, you'll make money on the deal.

Flip This House

The Dangers of Flipping

Most people have heard the term "flip" in the context of investment real estate. You often hear someone say that they want to go out and "flip" a property. Flipping is basically buying a property, rehabbing, and then selling for a profit.

Sounds good...on paper.

Is it a viable strategy? Yes, but a few words of caution here.

The first thing you need to be aware of is one of the **dumbest** laws or so-called laws in the history of mankind. In certain parts of the country you have to wait a certain period of time before you can re-sell a property. This is called "seasoning" and the timeline is usually 90 days.

Why do I think this is dumb? Well, it is **your** property...you **own** it, and yet you are being told what you can do with **your** property. That's enough on that. My rant on this subject could fill an entire book. It is what it is, so be sure of any "seasoning guidelines" in your area.

The other thing you need to be **very** aware of, as always, is the property values in the area. At the time of this writing, most of the country has bottomed out on values and they are now on the way up. This leads to potential danger because it circumvents Rule Number 1 in this business, which is… "You make your money when you **buy** not when you **sell**!"

That means, we buy **below** market value.

With market conditions as they are today in many parts of the country, you are often buying at the **top** of the market and hoping to make your money on the appreciation.

Remember this phrase, "HOPE IS A VERY POOR FINANCIAL STRATEGY!"

As a matter of fact, that strategy of buying at the top and hoping to make profit on appreciation is exactly what sent so many inexperienced investors to the poor house a few years back.

That being said, due to the historic downturn, and the values dropping so low, in many parts of the country, it would be a safe bet to employ this strategy as long as you **know** what you are doing.

For instance, as of September 2012, the Phoenix area, which was one of the top three hardest hit areas of the country, has gone up in value 28% with values still **well below** the historic highs.

If you were in a market similar to this, that would make it a fairly safe bet to buy based on appreciation.

The Basics of Flipping

When you plan on flipping a house you have to evaluate it just as carefully as if you were going to rehab it for a rental. You still have to make your money on the purchase, so it has to be a smart buy. You still run down all the leads you've gotten from your Realtor and you've narrowed things down to a few choices. We'll cover this in a little more detail in the next chapter, *Do Your Homework.*

Something you all must learn to do is to document what you're looking at, document the properties you're considering. That way, when you sit down to make your choice, you have side-by-side comparisons of the properties.

When you're evaluating a property to flip, you want to be systematic. Look at all aspects of each and every home. Hopefully your Realtor will have provided you with a listing sheet, but that doesn't have all the information you're looking for. Make your own notes, take your own measurements, and write down your own opinions about things that might need attention.

If you don't take these steps, you won't put in the right offer, and you'll lose money.

Some of my students take cameras with them so they can take photos of the properties. Make a note of the image number and what the image is so that when you get home you can put it with the right property sheet.

Some students will take a digital recorder or use their phone and record their notes as they're going through the properties. In our courses, we provide you with all these sheets and checklists.

What to Consider

You consider everything. Start by looking at the outside of the property and evaluate the walkways, driveway, stairs, porches, and decks. How does the lawn look? The trees, flowers, and shrubs? Any problems with traffic, getting in and out of a driveway? Any concerns about the siding, the roof, etc. should be noted before going into the residence. That way, if there looks to be a roof issue, you can look for evidence of it inside.

Now head inside the property and start from the bottom and go up, or start at the top and go all the way down to the basement. *Evaluate everything.* Walls, ceilings, doors, windows, flooring, lighting fixtures, electrical outlets and their placement, fireplaces, wood stoves, closets, gas or electric, water softeners, etc.

Do the kitchens and bathrooms have GCFI electric outlets, ventilation? How well do the faucets work, water pressure, is there a water meter? One Case Study will tell you about a property that the bank had to drop radically in price because the house didn't have its own water meter; it had shared one with a neighboring house because when both houses were built, they were family members.

Have you noticed any signs of water damage? Does it match with your observations you made outside about the roof or siding? Check the A/C units, the furnace, water heater, electrical box, and if you don't know what you're looking for, find out. Don't make this trip a waste of your time.

As you get going in this industry, you're going to hear other investors say, "The rougher they are the better I like them." What many novice real estate investors see as a disaster, the seasoned professional sees as serious opportunity. When you know what you're looking for, profit starts to appear in the most unlikely places.

Fast Road to Riches

This is the only place in the book I'm going to talk about "fast" anything in terms of generating wealth. I put that title in there because I knew it would attract your attention.

Now that I have it, here's the deal:

HIRE OUT THE REHAB WORK!

I'm serious here. This is one of the biggest mistakes novice real estate investors make when they start investing. They say, "I'm pretty handy with a hammer, I can fix this place up in no time."

In no time, huh?

Are you already independently wealthy? Have you quit your job already? Are you nuts?

This is one of the first rules most of my students break and they all come back to me and tell me that I'm right. They started the rehab project and then life happened. They had to work overtime, the baby got sick, a wife/husband had to take care of a sick parent.

You name it and life's going to throw it at you.

And all that time the clock is ticking, ticking, ticking away. Every day you don't get something done on that house is money going down the toilet. Every week your property isn't ready is another week's rent you aren't collecting.

That's not the point of investment real estate!

If you want a hobby, go ahead, buy a fixer-upper and spend the next two or three years getting it fixed up. Just don't tell people you're a real estate investor when you do this, because you're not.

Pay a good, qualified contractor to handle the rehab.

Once you find a good one, you stick with him. Don't make the same mistake I did and hire the first one you find in the paper, in the phone book, or on Craig's list. Check them out, and I mean thoroughly. Ask to see their last ten or twenty properties. Ask for references, from last week, last month, last year. Anyone can get lucky once or twice, but a good contractor will have a whole list of happy clients you can use to validate before hiring.

Not so Fast – Sweat Equity

All right. You don't have a whole lot of money, and you really want/need to do the work yourself. Consider, then exactly how much it is going to cost you to do the entire project yourself. And when you're sanding window sills, chipping up stubborn tile, or baffled by a light that turns off when the switch is turned on, ask yourself if it's worth the money you're saving. How much do you earn at work?

Are you really making that much fixing the house up yourself?

In some cases, there might be things you can do to save on the cost of rehabbing. Perhaps you love painting, or doing tile work. Some of my students claim to really love that stuff. That's great, then do it.

But if you realize that you are holding back the project, then your sweat equity could be costing you some money. What you might need to look for is a rehab project where you can do some of the work, but then you hire out the rest. But you have to keep up the pace, because you want a property rehabbed within a matter of a couple weeks, not a couple months or worse, a couple of years.

Contractors who really know what they're doing make it look so easy. Just turn on the Do it Yourself shows on television. It used to be that those shows absolutely drove me nuts because they never showed how frustrating and agonizing it can be to do a rehab when you don't know what you're doing.

Now, because of the popularity of reality TV today, there are shows where couples try to rehab a kitchen or bathroom over the course of a week. They spend an entire week working on the project and run into wall after wall after wall because they don't have the necessary expertise, tool, equipment, or part.

Most of the projects eventually get done, but not until the couples end up hating each other. In some cases, they have to call in a professional and fix what they messed up. Every single one of the shows interviews the couples and they all say the same thing, "I've never worked so hard in my life. I would never do that again."

So, sweat equity can be a good thing, but be sure that's really the way you want to go.

I figure I'm worth more than $10 to $20 an hour, so I'd rather pay someone else to do that work, and then when the work's done and I sell the house I take a great big check to the bank and I'm happy.

I say, "I LOVED doing that. I think I'll do it again!"

Do Your Homework

Check the Neighborhood

In one of the Case Studies, one of my students says, "If I don't feel comfortable leaving my wife there alone during the rehab project, then I don't want the property."

That's an important instinct to listen to. If you feel that the neighborhood is unsafe, how do you think your potential tenants or buyers will feel? You might have the most wonderfully renovated house on the block, but if the neighborhood is unsafe, you will not be able to get the kind of tenants that make investors happy...you know the kind...the ones who have jobs and pay on time every month.

If, however, you have a neighborhood that is mostly single family homes, and there appear to be a lot of young families living there, then that one single house that has sat abandoned for a long time might be an excellent purchase. The neighborhood is already a good neighborhood, and the neighbors will be really happy that you cleaned up the property. It will improve their home values, and it will attract the kind of tenants/buyers you are looking for.

Other things to consider too are access to public transportation, schools, churches, and shopping.

If you're looking to attract young professionals, they will likely be more interested in nearby night-life, not necessarily a quiet neighborhood. If you're looking to attract young families, then a quiet neighborhood near churches and schools might fit the bill better.

This is when it is good to have a very knowledgeable Realtor working for you. If they know the neighborhoods and the needs of the potential tenants/buyers, they will be able to give you really good advice on how you should consider approaching your renovation.

Location

Sometimes investors are swayed into making an unwise purchase because the property is priced very low because of its location. Often a bad location equals a very low asking price.

There are investors who see this as an opportunity to make a difference in the neighborhood by improving a single house; they could potentially change the entire neighborhood. But make sure you take into consideration the risk involved.

What if you rehab the property, it's the nicest house on the block now, but no one else has done anything to improve their properties? You have no influence there. You may end up having to take lower rent or selling it for a lower price than you had anticipated because of this.

Before you buy a property priced low because of its location, evaluate how you can change things to make the property more appealing. If the change is a simple matter, perhaps putting up a privacy fence, it might be worth considering. If it is something that cannot be changed, like being located next to a very busy highway, you may want to reconsider your purchase.

One of the projects that I encourage is to get a group of investors together and revamp an entire neighborhood. This can easily be done in neighborhoods where prices are very low because the entire neighborhood needs to be rehabbed.

Once everything has been rehabbed, then it changes the market for those investors.

What Can YOU Change?

As a real estate investor, you will be looking at investment properties differently than you would for properties you would purchase for your own use. As a result, you find yourself willing to overlook a number of objectionable things such as holes in the walls, leaky faucets, stained carpeting, etc.

But, what you *cannot* do is change views, locations, access to roadways, etc.

If there is a problem with the property that you cannot change, be ready to walk away. A good investment always makes sense. You don't have to talk yourself into it.

When you're talking yourself into something, that's a warning sign.

If it is out of your control, walk away.

Ready to Be a Landlord?

Residential Real Estate

From the point of my first solo purchase where I made money even after dealing with a number of unscrupulous professionals I just kept going. I kept buying and selling properties. Then I got into rental properties and I learned another valuable lesson.

I didn't know how to be a landlord.

So, my tenants taught me how to be a landlord.

This is probably the number one thing that keeps people from getting involved in real estate. They don't want to be a landlord. I did because in order to have these properties I had to build my portfolio.

Again, without education and training, I had to learn things the hard way. My tenants taught me their way by doing what they wanted when they wanted. They paid when the felt like paying, and when they didn't feel like paying, they didn't. They would give me every excuse in the book as to why they didn't have their money and if I decided to evict them, they would destroy the property.

Remember, at this time I was still trying to educate myself about real estate investing, and one of the tapes I was listening to featured an old-time landlord who managed hundreds of properties. He said, "Here's my advice for anyone who wants to be a landlord, if you can't evict someone on Christmas Eve, you're not cut out to be a landlord."

That seemed to be pretty harsh to me. Until my own problem tenant cropped up.

My problem tenant was a veteran, a really nice guy, a *great* guy. He paid his first month's rent on time, but each month he kept getting later and later. He'd have one excuse after another, but I wanted to believe in the buy because he was so nice. It turned out that he was running a major drug operation out of his apartment. I had to evict him...and he threatened to have me disappear.

So much for him being a great guy.

Can You Evict Someone on Christmas Day?

I figured I'd learned my lesson and it would never happen again.

Just a little while later the couple in the front apartment fall behind on their rent and are giving me every excuse in the book. Those words, "If you can't evict someone on Christmas Eve..." kept running through my head, because it's December. I had to file with the magistrate to have these tenants evicted and I won.

The next step is to have a constable come and help you evict them if they don't leave willingly.

It was December 23 and the constable said, "You gotta be kidding! It's Christmas. You can't throw them out."

I said, "I just know they're not going to pay. I want them out."

The constable said, "Let me talk to them. I'm sure they'll pay." He came out a few minutes later and said, "They promise to pay you right after the first of the year.

Against my better judgment I allowed the constable to convince me not to kick them out right before Christmas. Come the first of the year, not only haven't they paid me, they've kicked holes in the walls, stripped plumbing out, and destroyed the apartment.

This was the last time I was going to let someone, who I felt was a responsible person, tell me how to run my business.

And that *was* the last time. It has never happened to me since.

Now, what I teach is that there are no excuses for not having your rent. We treat our tenants like gold, and so when it comes time to pay their rent, the ones who appreciate having a nice place to live pay us right away. We tell them that we will take care of them and they will love where they live. However, if they don't pay, there is no excuse. Unless they're dead, there is no excuse. They laugh at that, but I tell them I'm not kidding.

I have heard *every* excuse in the book...every last one of them. But you know what? My bank doesn't want to hear excuses because they're looking for their money and I'm the one on the line when it isn't there. It's an agreement.

My approach is to file an eviction notice as soon as is allowable by law. That gets their attention and they usually call us asking what's going on. I say, "Have you sent your rent? Because we don't have it yet. Until we get it, we have to continue with the eviction process."

That is how to make sure your tenants pay, and pay on time. We treat our tenants like gold and in return we expect them to pay on time and keep their rental property in good condition.

Section 8 Housing

Some real estate investors don't like to worry about renting to Section 8 people, and others love it. Personally, I love it. Because it is a federally funded program to assist low-income families, the elderly, and the disabled to afford safe and clean housing.

Anyone who qualifies for Section 8 is allowed to find their own housing, and this includes single-family homes, townhouses, and apartments. They are free to choose any housing that meets the requirements of the program.

FYI, this is different from subsidized housing.

Section 8 renters can rent from the private sector. As a real estate investor, a Section 8 tenant is guaranteed rent because the government puts the check into your account every month, on time, every time. You never have to worry whether their rent will be paid or not.

If you are interested in renting to Section 8 tenants, you will have to be approved by the program and the property will need to pass an annual inspection to make sure you are keeping it maintained, clean, and safe.

The reason this is so valuable is that when you are dealing with lower income housing or more affordable housing, you won't have to worry with the economy falling if your tenants are going to be able to pay you the rent.

There are certain specifications that must be met, and some real estate investors don't want to deal with the hassle of that. Other real estate investors absolutely love renting to Section 8 people and often have a waiting list of interested parties. Once the word about your good properties gets out, you may never worry about finding tenants ever again.

Evaluating a Property

A good way to get started in this business is to pick one type of investing and get really good at it. I know people who specialize in single family homes and have never done anything else. They managed to find their niche and they are very comfortable and very successful at it.

Problems or Potential?

When you go to look at a potential investment property for the first time, it is often good to go in the company of some of the hovels I show them as potential investment properties and they stare at the property, their mouths hanging open. "Are you *kidding* me?"

The property often looks abandoned, the paint peeling, often the windows are broken, or cracked. The landscape is either overgrown or the lawn is dead.

Then we go inside and it looks even worse. The walls might have huge holes ripped into them, and the copper pipe might be missing from the plumbing system. Copper has been selling for pretty high prices, and empty homes are often the likeliest source.

Carpets can be ripped and stained with all manner of substances. Cabinets in the kitchens and bathrooms might be missing doors and handles and usually the appliances are also missing.

Where new investors see disastrous problems, I see huge potential. The worse a property looks, the lower my bid. If the seller is motivated enough, often because there hasn't been a single bid in months, I get the property for a nicely low price, and after figuring in my rehab costs, I know what I can reasonably expect to make when I go to sell that property.

Most novice investors will either overestimate or underestimate how much it will cost to renovate and rehab a house. That is why it is critical to have those numbers with you when you go to visit a house.

I say this over and over again, "The numbers never lie."

If a property is priced properly and you make a good estimation of the rehab costs, you will make your money with the purchase, which is where you should *always* make it.

KNOW Your NUMBERS

When you know your numbers, you've plugged them in and they say that the property you're looking at is a good investment, remember to not sit and wait for a week to "think about it."

While you're thinking about it, someone else is going to come along and snap it up.

I've said it before and I'll say it again, "The numbers don't lie."

You know the price of the home, you have a worksheet that lists all the things that need to be done during the rehab. Based on this list, you deduct certain things from your offer. Yes, this is how you make your money on the purchase. The home is in bad shape, but the bank/owner is still looking to get as much out of it as possible. When you run into someone who refuses to be reasonable about your offer, walk away. There'll be another opportunity tomorrow.

Comps

Once you've made a decision to look at a few properties with your Realtor, make sure to look at all the pertinent comps (comparables) so that you can see how much you can reasonably expect to realize from the sale of the house. If this home is about the same size, age, and condition of the other houses on the comp list, then you know immediately how much you can sell the house for.

This is very important!

Comparable means comparable.

Apples to apples.

This means if a home down the street sold for $200,000 in ten days and you want the same result for your potential property, you need to find out **exactly** what that home had inside.

You have to know the types of kitchen, bathrooms, room sizes, age, finish, new carpet, paint, etc. Determine if you can do the same thing to yours or maybe even just a little bit better.

Here's an example where newbie investors make big mistakes:

Let's say the check a comparable to their property, and the comparable says that it has a brand-new kitchen. "OK," says the newbie investor. "I need to put in a brand-new kitchen. But the newbie puts in a brand-new starter kitchen with entry level cabinets, countertops, floor, and appliances. But their comparable house had solid cherry cabinets, full granite countertops, and top of the line flooring and appliances.

They are both brand-new kitchens.

But they are **not** comparable.

This type of mistake can, and will, make or break your deal.

Ideally, we want comparable sales within the last 30 days, no further out if possible. The absolute maximum is 90 days. Six month old comparables don't cut it. They will cause an issue with the appraisal and with the bank.

A seasoned Real Estate agent accustomed to working with investors will know the value of the most recent comps. If your agent says they can only find six month old comps, find a new agent.

Do the NUMBERS Add Up?

OK, here is the formula I strongly suggest that you live by.

This formula will eliminate any fears you have about missing anything in your rehab estimates, etc. by giving you the absolute top number you should offer for any given property:

MAO = ARV – 30% – Repair Costs

- MAO – Maximum Allowable offer
- ARV – After Repair Value
- 30% is the profit margin or spread you wish to make

We normally want to start our bid 10 – 15% below our maximum allowable offer

This is why it is so important to know your comparable sales. You **must** know the ARV (After Repair Value) of the property. We don't care what it is worth right now, or what they are asking for. We are only concerned with how much it will be worth if I do, X, Y, and Z.

You may be saying to yourself, "Jim, they'll never take an offer that low. That is pennies on the dollar!"

My answer is, "You're right, it is. That's how you make money."

I don't care if they say no. this is just a numbers game. If you put enough offers in, your pennies on the dollar offer will eventually be accepted. This formula allows you not only bit profit potential, but safety.

If you are operating off a potential $30,000 profit, somehow, someway there was a $10,000 mistake you missed, you still have $20,000 left.

If you're operating off a potential $10,000 profit and the same issue occurs, you now either broke even, or worse, are losing money.

Remember, this is just a numbers game. Pennies on the dollar offers are accepted all the time, you just need to get your offers in.

Price You Pay

When you look at a property and see its listed value, does this mean you have to offer that price.

No!

This is where it gets fun.

Based on your evaluation sheet, you mark down absolutely everything you will have to repair or replace in order to effectively bring the property up to the standard of the neighborhood.

If the furnace looks old, it probably is. Deduct the cost of a new furnace from your bid. How does the roof look? When you can take something off the asking price, do it.

Going into negotiations, I ask for the moon and a lot of times I get it.

Because the furnace has to be replaced or the roof is not looking good, I might knock off money from their asking price. I might put in very, very low bid. If they take it, super! If they don't, I might renegotiate, or I walk.

I have to know that I am going to make money on this deal. If I don't have a chance of making money, then I don't waste their time, and I don't let them waste mine.

Refurb Prices

Here's where you have to have an excellent contractor you can trust as part of your team. In order to know if your numbers work, you must make a very close estimate on the refurb costs.

If you over-estimate the refurb costs, you might walk away from a really sweet deal because of your ignorance.

If you under-estimate the refurb costs, you might get yourself into a losing proposition, but not realize it until you're firmly in the middle of it. Your only choice might be to sell at a loss having learned an expensive lesson.

Your worksheet should include the cost of everything from how much it costs to drywall/prep/paint a room to how much it will cost to replace all or part of a roof. You can't guess here. You have to approximate the costs based on information you have gotten from your contractor.

Types of Investing

You never go into a deal without knowing how you're going to get out.

You plan to either buy and sell, buy and hold, lease option, or wholesale.

Your investing style depends entirely on what you want to do, what your overall goals in real estate investing are and your plan to get there.

Flip

Some people are not interested in accumulating assets. They just want to make some extra money.

These people will gravitate toward doing a flip. You have to be pretty well targeted to do a flip. You must know the neighborhood and get the right kind of work done.

Done well, flips are an excellent way to raise money quickly either to pay off other debt or to give you more working capital for your real estate investing.

Rental Portfolios

Some people want to build rental portfolios, which is one approach that I recommend because there is the old saying, "Don't wait to buy real estate. Buy real estate and wait." People who get into this game today are going to be so happy they did ten years from now!

Wholesaling

A lot of people with no money and no credit like to do wholesale deals. Typically they're finding a deal, putting it under contract and they selling that contract to another investor who is interested in buying it. You never have to put any money down on it. Once the person buys the contract off you, you're done. The rest is up to them. In the case of wholesaling, it helps to have several potential buyers lined up, that way if one isn't interested, the next one will be.

There are ways to protect yourself by using option contracts so you can get out of it if you can't find a buyer.

Part II

The Guide to Real Estate Investment SCAMS

Real Estate Investing

This term puts the fear of God in most people. Just tell someone you're going to go into real estate investing, and you are going to hear all kinds of advice, nearly all of it negative:

"You'll lose your shirt."

"You don't know what you're getting into."

"Those real estate courses are nothing but a scam."

"What, are you crazy? Put your money into the stock market! At least that's safe!"

Are these statements true?

Yes, they really could be. I know, that's a pretty strange thing to admit in a book that is designed to get you interested in real estate investing. What I want you to understand is that real estate investing is a business, and when you do your due diligence, you can really make a great living at it.

But...if you don't, you could lose your shirt and you will end up believing that the course you purchased **was** a scam.

I talked with Andrew Waite, publisher of **Personal Real Estate Investor Magazine**, a publication designed to inform the savvy investor the truth of the current real estate market.

Andrew had a few things to say about real estate investing courses that you really should know about.

Who Are You Working With?

When you consider investing in someone's program and you call for information, ask who you're talking to, ask for their full name.

Many real estate investing gurus have a boiler-room in Utah answering their calls and you will never, *ever* get the chance to speak to the person who is offering the real estate investing course. Instead, you're talking to some hireling who is being paid minimum wage to talk you into a program.

Then you need to ask if the person selling the real estate investing program has any experience at real estate investing. You would be amazed at the number of real estate investing gurus who have actually never bought real estate in their lives, and these include some very big, very well-known names.

Most of the time the people you end up talking to on the phone are hired under the guise of giving advice, but they're only paid an hourly fee plus a commission if they sell you into a program.

These people have been very, very well trained, using carefully crafted scripts peppered with neurolinguistic programming to cajole and lull you into making a purchase. Their intention is to con you into separating you from your hard-earned money, and believe me, they know how to do it.

Unfortunately, there are a lot of scammy people in this profession. As a consumer, you need to be aware of what you're going to get for the money they're asking. The problem with this industry is that there is no standard for what is being sold.

How Do Scams Work?

Here's what you need to know:

A number of people set themselves up as real estate investment educators. You've seen the television ads. They use the promise of wealth, show several well-endowed blondes, a pool, and palm trees. They promise a "No Money Down" or "Little Money Down" method of accumulating great wealth.

These commercials promise a dream that is so appealing that those who are most at risk are the ones who answer the ads. It is not the sophisticated, educated potential investor who has worked hard, has money, and manages it carefully.

The promise of fast and easy wealth targets the gullible, those who are on their last legs; the vulnerable retirees, and those desperate people who have fallen out of American corporate life.

These people are looking for an easy way to achieve this dream, a quick way back to wealth and riches. They desperately want the scam to be real.

Listen carefully to the language of these commercials. The language is designed to persuade you to come to a meeting where a well-known celebrity will show you how to make a fortune in real estate investing.

These introductory meetings are designed to get you to come back for another meeting, a paid meeting this time. And that more expensive meeting is designed to get you into an even more expensive meeting, weekend seminar, or week-long bootcamp where you will "learn everything you need to know about..."

They may even promise that for the next meeting you can bring your wife/husband/partner for free. This is designed to make you think that you're getting a great deal for your money.

Once you give them money for that next meeting, weekend, or bootcamp, they will flatter you, support you, stay in touch with you because they want to keep you happy and not cancel your agreement.

Plastic Celebrity

You'll pick up a magazine or newspaper and see an ad with the face of a famous celebrity who will be in town, giving a presentation on how to get involved in their real estate investing education program.

Most of these meetings imply that you will be attending a meeting that will be run by the celebrity featured in the ad. None of these celebrities are found at any of these events. Instead, the event will be run by a group of people that have been hired to facilitate the meeting or event.

Here is what you will experience:

You will call an 800 number to sign up for the event, which will be held in a B-rate hotel conference. At the hotel, the doors to the event will be closed and outside those closed doors will be a registration table where your name will be checked off. You may be issued a name tag by the people behind the table who don't seem terribly connected with what they're doing. They're not quite as well trained as the people you will meet inside the room.

Outside the door will be a pop-up sign with a picture of the celebrity that you will all be looking at as you mill about, wondering what to do next. The doors are still closed, and they won't let you in until the minute the seminar is scheduled to start. Everyone attending the event will cluster around the doors and table while those behind the table continue to register more people.

At the advertised time, the doors open with a flourish.

- The first thing you will notice is that there will be very loud, energizing music playing.
- The second thing you will see is another larger-than-life poster cut-out of the celebrity you expected to be presenting.
- And the third thing you will notice is that the room will be very cold.

At the back of the room will be a table. Everyone will file past this table. As you find seats at the back of the room, you will be told to move to the front so that as more people come in late they won't disturb those of you who were kind enough to be on time for the presentation.

What they're doing is front-loading the room.

They know no one else is coming, most of the people who registered have already been checked off the list. There will be a projector and a screen at the front of the room. You still don't know who will be presenting.

Then, a very good-looking, successful-appearing young man will get up and thank you for coming. He will then apologize for not having the celebrity there, but they will play a video of the celebrity talking to you. Sometimes the celebrity will appear to be speaking to the person who welcomed you, introducing the presenter as the celebrity's new "assistant" or "friend" or "partner" and encourage you to listen to everything the presenter has to say.

The truth is, the celebrity is **never** in attendance.

They just use that to rope you in, as a way to get people into the room. Who you are actually listening to is someone who has licensed that person's name to use for the purposes of promoting whatever real estate investing education they're hoping to sell.

Later, when you go back and look at the ad or promotion that got you to the event, it will say, "Celebrity will not necessarily be in attendance."

What you need to know is that all the people at this presentation are paid actors or well-educated administrators who have had a great deal of practice at presenting this material. The one who is doing all the presenting is typically an actor.

All these groups are in the business of selling education, and after they get your money, they have no interest of you actually succeeding in the program.

There is no investment in you.

After the recorded message from the promised celebrity, the actor will give you his pitch and his whole game is to get people to go to the back of the room, to that table back there, (the one between you and the exit) to sign up and pay some money for the next event. Their goal is to typically get a ten to twenty percent conversion.

If there are one hundred people in the room, they hope to get ten people signed up for the next event, which will cost from $1,500 to $3,000, but could cost as much as $40,000 to $75,000 in some cases. This means they have made at least $30,000 in a single hour.

Typically they have two presentations at a single location, one in the late afternoon, and then a second one later in the evening. Between the two, they will have made about $60,000 for that event at that one location.

In a larger metropolitan area, they will run six of these presentations over the course of three days, so they can expect to clear at least a quarter million dollars in a single weekend.

The Powerful Close – The "Set-Up"

During the presentation, you will be "trained" to respond quickly. In complete honesty, you're being set up. These people are very well trained to set up the audience to close a sale, and in order to do that, you will be set up.

You will be made to feel that their offer is so good that you'd be an idiot to pass it up. One such set-up is they will have a book that they're recommending you need to read. They will walk around the front during their presentation, holding the book up high, gesturing with it, telling you how much good information is in that book. Then they will stop and ask, "What are **you** willing to do to get your hands on this book?

Unless you've heard of this set-up before, almost everyone in attendance will be thinking hard to come up with an original idea. Finally, either someone in the audience will figure it out, or a plant in the audience will jump up, run to the front of the room and grab the book out of the presenter's hand.

The presenter will get very excited and say, "Now, **that's** what I'm talking about! You have to **grab** the opportunity when it presents itself!"

This is designed to get everyone else in the audience to kick themselves for not grabbing that opportunity.

They've just been set up.

Now, when the next "great opportunity" is presented, more people in the audience will jump up and run to the back of the room because they've been conditioned to act without thinking.

They will be told, "This is a limited time offer, and only the first five people who sign up will get this very special price for themselves and one additional person!"

These people are very, very good at manipulating your emotions. Even people who know what to expect find themselves wanting to respond. They have to steel themselves from reacting.

Once you've signed up, the company is going to embark on a heavy telemarketing program that is run out of one of those boiler-rooms in Salt Lake City. This program is designed to make sure you "stick" with the commitment you have made. They call everyone who signed up, tell them how smart they are to have taken advantage of the opportunity, how impressed they are with your intelligence and savvy. They will do everything in their power to keep you from backing out of your decision.

You will be made to feel very, very special until they get all the money out of you they can possibly get.

Then, you'll never hear from them again.

Getting More Credit

In some cases, once you attend the next event, you will be assigned a mentor or a counselor. One of their tricks is to get you to call your credit card companies asking for a raise in your credit limit. You may even be encouraged to do this for all your credit cards, and this new amount of money you have available will be recorded on your sheet.

The next program they advise for you will cost just about as much money as you managed to get out of your credit cards.

Effectively, this has put you into a position of drowning in debt again, and once they have all the money they can squeeze out of you, they don't care about your success.

You will also not have any money to put toward your investments. You might have gotten some education, but you're cash and credit poor now.

How to Protect Yourself

Before you part with your money, do your "due diligence." Find out who you will be learning from. Ask that person if they have actually bought investment real estate. Where? What are the addresses? How many deals have you done in the past few years?

Then find out what you are going to get for your money. Is there a money back guarantee? What do you have to do to qualify for that refund? What will you learn? What can you expect to be able to do once you've completed your education?

Separate yourself from the emotional response generated by the ad or the presentation. Make sure you research the person or group who is advertising the free presentation.

When you attend my presentation, I am there. I'm the one doing the presenting. Many times, when I introduce myself to some of the attendees, their response is, "You're Jim Toner? I never expected to see you here!"

At my presentation, I tell you what you can do to change your lives by getting into investment real estate. I also tell you exactly how much it is going to cost, and what you can expect to get out of the program. I have a money back guarantee that is easy for me, because if you do what you've been taught to do, you will be successful.

Once you become my student, you are a forever student. Any time you have a question, all you have to do is call, and you will get the answer you're looking for. I am deeply conscious of how precious your money is, and the last thing I am going to do is waste either your money or your time. I don't resort to tricks because I don't have to.

Your success is my success.

Part III

Rather than having me go on and on about my experiences, I want you to hear from some of our students. Each case study you read will help you to see that getting into investment real estate does not require that you be a rocket scientist.

You will be pleased to know that one of the case studies highlights the investment real estate activities of a young 24-year-old investor, and that the 12-year-old son of one other investor has already mastered the ability to assess the condition of a house.

It's like I told you at the beginning of this book, I was the only one who was keeping me from being successful in investment real estate. Once I got past that, everything fell into place. As you read through this section, you will see how easy it can be to incorporate investing in real estate into your daily lives.

You will hear from the following real estate investors:

- Bruce Rhiel
- Ed Perez
- Dave and Irina
- Evan Mendelhall
- Josh Meeder
- Ken George
- Staci and Derrik Kuhns

Case Study – Bruce Rhiel

Full-time Real Estate Investor

Becoming a real estate investor was easier than I ever expected it to be. You don't have to have tons of money or know-how. You just have to know where to get the answers and to proceed properly.

I'm a full-time real estate investor, having quit my job, so I guess I've done a lot of things right.

Unlike a number of people, I was not flat broke and barely making it when I decided to enter this field. I was actually doing quite well. I had a great job as a mechanical engineer and my wife was a manager at a vision clinic, so it's not like we were destitute.

I had a pretty good background. I was born in a rural community, so I did a lot of hands-on things and my wife and I together built our own house. We built a pretty nice sized house, so I had a good background as far as knowing how to frame it, doing the construction type things, how to wire, etc..

Being an engineer is actually a pretty good job. It is mostly sitting in an air-conditioned office, but I always felt that I just wanted something more in my life. My wife would laugh at me saying that I had a five-year itch. The longest I held an engineering job was about five years, so I guess you could say she was right. I found I got tired of my job, and would want to move on and I would find another engineering job. They were all good jobs. But, I just wanted something different.

I used to tell people, my very first real estate deal was the house we bought. We bought 21 acres with the idea of building houses on it. We paid $30,000 for it. We thought that was about the going price and later I sold off 12 acres of it for $69,500 and I used that money to build my house.

However, I first dabbled in real estate investing when I initially bought a fourplex and a duplex. I discovered later that I could have really gotten burned on those deals, but instead I lucked out. There was a fellow I knew who wanted to sell them and we purchased them on a land contract.

To tell you how much of a rookie I was, I never even walked into some of the units. I bought them sight unseen!

He said he wanted to sell both of the units for $175,000 and I thought that sounded like a good deal, but I had no clue as to running comparables, or doing anything to make sure I wasn't cheated.

I just did it.

Later, when we got the properties appraised, one of them appraised for $141,000, and the second one appraised for $120,000. So that ended up being one heck of a deal for me. I paid $175,000 for both properties and when they were appraised two years later, they appraised for about $260,000.

Meanwhile I sold that 12 acres, took that money and invested in the stock market and figured I could grow that by the time I got ready to sell my house. But I lost it, not quite all of it, but I lost a lot of it. That is when the light clicked on for me.

I picked real estate investing as my avenue.

What really did it for me was an infomercial of all things. It was the middle of the night. My brother had read the book *Rich Dad, Poor Dad* by Robert Kiyosaki and passed it on to my mother and they both thought it was just great. I just never had time to sit down and read, so one night, during an infomercial, Robert Kiyosaki came on and he was advertising his program, "Choose to Be Rich". That was the thing that triggered it for me.

His whole message was "You can choose to be rich if you want to, it's a choice." If you want to be rich, you just have to do the steps required to get there.

I attended one of Kiyosaki's presentations at the Lawrence Convention Center. While I was there, I saw Jim Toner's booth set up there to discuss his program. My wife and I both signed up to take his class. I realized that my first real estate deals were pretty lucky, but now it was time for me to formalize my training in real estate. There was a lot that I did not know. I'd been doing a lot of reading and trying to learn things on my own. I realize I'd been lucky in my first deals.

Shortly after that, my employer was starting to lay off engineers.

No, I'm not going to tell you I was one who lost my job. Actually, I **wanted** them to lay me off, but they wouldn't. My employer wanted to move me into the graphic arts department because they knew I did pencil drawings. They wanted to keep me on, but not in engineering.

Now, there was going to be a bit of a pay cut and I said that I would really rather be laid off. We went back and forth for a while because they really wanted to keep me on. Finally, they listened and eventually they laid me off.

It allowed me to collect unemployment for a little while as I made that transition from a regular paycheck to doing investing.

The first few months went along OK. I took Jim's class in the spring and it was about nine months later that I left my job. I say I quit my job because I really did want to leave. I was trying to figure out the right time to do it. When this all happened...it was an easy transition for me.

Strangely enough, it really wasn't scary for me. I don't have much of a fear when it comes to that kind of thing. You hear a lot of people who are afraid to pull the trigger. Now, after fifty houses, nothing really bothers me.

There are a lot of people who think that having done fifty houses, I'm pretty much an expert, but I still find that there is something to be learned in this business every day. I went to a seminar a couple months ago and there was a young guy there who had bought 600 houses last year alone. Compared to him, I consider myself to be a novice.

But, compared to the average person who buys and sells less than six houses in their lifetime, and they've lived in all those houses, I guess I know a little more about real estate investing than they do.

Getting Started

Initially, I didn't really have any money to work with. At that time, you could use hard money lenders and I got really good at working their system. I had several hard-money lenders that I worked with and I could do the deals start to finish with no money out of my pocket at all.

Things were really going great until the economy hit. The hard-money lender thing is something I don't do at all anymore.

About that time, Jim Toner opened up several schools like the one he had in Pittsburgh and he asked me to be one of his instructors. As his instructor you are a mentor to new students. As a mentor, I work side-by-side with students and do walk-through deals and steer them on the right path.

One of my students was a gentleman who was a retired medical doctor. He wanted me to be his mentor, and I was happy to say yes.

He really struggled with it. He was physically handicapped after a bad car accident. He had no knowledge at all on houses. The normal terminology was just foreign to him. At one point, he then asked me if I wanted to be his partner and I said, "Yes." That really was a blessing for me because he had access to a lot of funds. It just made buying and selling houses really easy because I never questioned whether I was going to have money or not to do deals.

As we sell houses, we use that profit to reinvest.

This is something that Jim encourages us to do is to develop a group of investors. In my case, I just needed this one guy because I had the knowledge and know-how and he had the money required. That was a really great partnership.

Things have changed a little bit in the recent past because we sold a lot of houses on land contracts. The value of the homes isn't what it was a few years ago, so one house that initially appraised for $95,000 is only worth about $70,000 now. Those particular investments require that I just ride it out and wait for the home values to come back up again. I know they will. But, that's one of the reasons that real estate investing isn't a get rich quick kind of business. It's a get rich slow and steady kind of business.

When I sat down to look at all the houses I've done, out of those 50 houses, I still own 31 of them. That's a lot of money to be sitting there, even if it is $10,000 profit on each one, that's a lot of money sitting there.

I hope to realize it in the near future.

Investing Preferences

Every person in investment real estate has a favorite type of property they like to buy. While I started with the fourplex and duplex, I've come to realize that I don't really like being a landlord. I just don't have the personality for it.

In order to be a good landlord, you need to have very strict rules, you have to follow your own rules and be on top of things a lot. In Pennsylvania, you can get a license and you can be a property manager. Here in Ohio, you have to be a licensed broker to be able to be a property manager.

That really stinks because all your real estate brokers out there did not get into business to be property managers, they wanted to buy and sell houses. So, when they opened up their property managing business, that is just a sideline and they just get somebody else to run it for them. Here in Ohio, it is very tough to find good property managers. I hired two so far and on those two properties I have more headaches than my own. They didn't do their job.

My brother has rental properties; he is very strict, very thorough, so right now I have hired him to do mine. So technically he's not a manager. The lease agreements are between me and the renter and not between him and them.

My brother is actually pretty tough. If the check is not there on a certain day, he's on the phone calling. If they cry the blues, that makes it real easy when he calls me up and tells me what they're saying and I can be strong and make the right decision.

But, if they were to call me up personally and say they'll have the money by next Friday, I'll usually say, "OK, we'll work with you."

Because of this, I try to stay away from the rental properties. I keep the ones that I have because they're the ones that are doing well.

My preference in investing is to buy the three bedroom, one-and-a-half bath homes. And the rougher the better.

If you get a house where the kitchen cabinets are marginal, then I don't like that. That means I can't rip them out and put new cabinets in and really increase the value of the house so that means that I have to leave them in.

I would rather the drywall be falling off of it, the mold everywhere, cabinets falling off of it, just as ugly as sin and drive those prices down. That way I buy the house at a very low price because then my rehab cost doesn't change very much. When the cabinets are so-so, it costs me the same to replace them as it would if they were destroyed.

When I buy a home in pretty bad shape, that's when you make out like a bandit. Why? Because when you turn around and sell that house, you show the before and after photos to the bank and they can see that the house was almost a total loss, and now, by putting in a new bathroom, new kitchen, brand new everything, the house now looks like a brand new home.

What You Shouldn't Do, But Can

I have an art background. The artistic part in me comes out a little bit as we're doing a rehab. We'll modify things, take out walls, open up doorways to give it that "open floor plan" feel. I think we do that more than most investors.

Another area where I'm different from other investors is I like to work on the color schemes and stage the homes. I really enjoy that part of the business. For the homes that I put up for sale, I always get some really good feedback from the Realtors who walk in.

Recently, we just completed my favorite deal to date. We bought two houses in one shot. There was a small ranch home that the parents were living in. Their son had come home and was building a 3000 square foot home. He had framed it in, installed some of the windows, and done some of the electric. Then he got a job in South Carolina and wanted to move his dad with him. So, I bought both houses on three acres for $60,000.

When we evaluated the situation, we saw that the house in back had a few walls in it, but they weren't laid out right. The guy didn't know what he was doing, so we pulled them out. Then I put those rusty engineering skills to use, used AutoCAD and I drew the whole house up from scratch. Everything was my lay-out.

The house is coming along really well and I'm anxious to see it completed.

I have one guy I've been using for quite a while who does the major contracting work for me.

There are certain things that I do go in and do myself. It depends on how busy I am at the time. There are a lot of days where my real estate business doesn't take up the same amount of time as a full-time job. So, if it works for me, I'll go in there and do some of the work myself.

But, most real estate investors, the ones who really know what they're doing, they'll tell you that you shouldn't ever be working on your own properties. They'll tell you that you're wasting your time because you're only making about $20 an hour and when you're doing the actually buying and selling you're making hundreds of dollars an hour.

I understand that.

It just depends on how busy I am and how many offers I have coming in and how much money I have to work with. So, I can work on it and save some rehab costs and earn a little bit of money on the side because my LLC will pay me to do that work.

The way it works is this, I come up with my rehab number and if I have tile work in there, which I can do well, I might do it myself. If I have a thousand dollars' worth of tile work in there, it will just pay me that thousand dollars. It will give me a little bit of spending money. I'll have two kids in college here pretty quick, so...I do some of the work. I can do all of it, I'm certainly capable of that.

However, I absolutely would **not** do **all** the rehab work.

Where I draw the line on that kind of behavior is if it will slow the project down by me doing the job. If that's the case, then I won't do it. If I feel I can get in there and get things done as fast as if I were going to be hiring a contractor, then I may do it.

The house we're doing, it has a master bathroom that has all kinds of tile in it. The shower is all tiled, the Jacuzzi tub...I took that project on because I'm cutting up the tile, I'm putting patterns in it and it's fairly fancy.

We're also doing a regular bathroom in tile and the foyer will also be tiled. That's a little more basic, so I'm thinking I'll hire someone to do those two jobs because if I were to do all three of them, I'll fall behind schedule.

The Perks of Real Estate Investing

When I was engineering, I will say, it was a good job. The atmosphere was nice, and I worked with really good people. But I tell people it's is like working on Saturdays. I wake up on a Saturday and if I **want** to do some work around the house, I do, but it isn't a job.

That's what it feels like to be a real estate.

Also, I'm not a morning person. I will work until 1:30 or 2:00 am, but I'm never up at 6:00 am. I never set my alarm clock. I wake up whenever I wake up. I like that freedom.

That's the very best thing about investment real estate, the freedom it has given me...if I don't make any more money at all, I would be willing to do it and make less money than I made in engineering and I would still do this because of that freedom that I have.

When my son started in 3rd grade, I wanted to coach the local youth football team. I've been doing it ever since. It takes a tremendous amount of time during leagues. My wife used to tell me she was a football widow. When football season came around, I just wasn't around. As a real estate investor, I could do that.

For the most part, when I want to take a day off, I just do it!

Being a real estate investor has given me the freedom to live life on my terms. There are some days when I don't feel like doing as much as other days.

Within reason...of course.

If there is a house that is waiting on me to get some things done, then I probably would not take much time off. But, if I wanted to, I could.

When I was working in "corporate America" I couldn't do that. You can't just call in to work day after day and say, "I'm not coming in today, I don't feel like working."

Investment real estate gave me the opportunity to be "the boss" without having to have employees. I had that experience once when I helped my parents out. They owned a small business and at one point in time they needed help. I quit my engineering job to help them run their business for a while. I loved the whole bit about being the boss, but I did **not** like having employees.

The whole time I did that I was trying to think of a business where I could be the boss without having employees. I wanted a business that would make money, provide a good living, and give me that time freedom I've been looking for. I found it in real estate investing.

I've been in real estate since about 2001 when I first bought those two rental properties. Part of me feels kind of silly because I bought those rental properties, made all kinds of money on them and yet didn't really jump into real estate investing until about 2005 when I decided to be a real estate investor.

What I Needed To Learn

When I first took Jim Toner's course, I learned a lot of technical things about real estate investing as far as how much things should cost. I knew how to drywall a room, but I had no clue how much it should cost to get it done. He had a spreadsheet already made out with dollar figures in it. For me, that was *huge*. It took all the guesswork out of things.

The other part of his program that I really liked was the mentorship part, and being connected with other like-minded people. There is a real estate investors association not far from where I live, but I won't go to that because all it is is a bunch of old guys who all have rental properties and they constantly complain about how bad things are. I can't stand listening to that.

If you go to one of Jim Toner's presentations, everyone is much more upbeat. It really keeps you involved, keeps your head on the right track. You're talking to other like-minded people. To me, that is huge!

There are times when you get a little discouraged and things aren't going the way you think they should be. Then you go talk to them and it helps your perspective.

I remember going to one of his meetings in particular. A woman was complaining about a nightmare deal she did. She shared all the details of how she bought it and wanted to sell it and couldn't get her money for it. She kept going on and on about how bad it was. In the end, she was renting the property and had a positive cash flow. In the end, she sold it and made a little bit of money in addition to the positive cash flow along the way.

Think about it! That was her nightmare story! Her nightmare was that she made money. Maybe not as much as she wanted, but she still made money.

I can tell you a nightmare story about investing in the stock market and losing twenty percent of my money. That wasn't even as bad as some people!

Her nightmare story was that she almost only broke even.

If you do your numbers right, and you do your homework, the chances of you actually losing money, are fairly small. Obviously, quite a few things can go wrong...you can spend more on rehab than you planned, your selling price might not be as high as you'd like, but there are a lot of things that help you to prevent those kinds of losses. You'd have to have a perfect storm, and even then you'll just be close to break-even.

If you recall my reference to the guy who bought 600 houses in one year; he buys homes in 33 states, and obviously he doesn't even see most of the houses. He has a team of people who do the buying and selling for him. He has a really strict set of rules that he expects all his people to work from. Recently he was going through all his numbers and he discovered that the least profitable deals were the ones he had handled. He was pretty rueful when he shared with me that he hadn't been following his own advice.

Once you come up with a system that works, you stick to it.

Most Common Mistakes

By far, the most common mistake most new real estate investors make is that they don't know their numbers.

They don't know the true rehab costs. They don't have a good idea of what their house should sell for based on the comparative values in the neighborhood.

Too many new real estate investors want to go with their gut feeling as to how much a house should sell for.

There's no room for gut feelings in real estate investing. The numbers don't lie. If the numbers are right you will make money. If they aren't, walk away from the deal.

Lack of education is another huge mistake. Without educating themselves on real estate investing, they're going to get burned.

I have a friend who decided to get into real estate investing without educating himself. He bought a house and is rehabbing it. He doesn't know what he's going to sell it for. They're putting a whole lot of money and time into this house on things that aren't going to add a dime to its value. This is a perfect example of not spending money wisely and getting emotionally attached to their rehab project rather than seeing it as a business project.

I'll admit that I struggle with that a bit myself. I'm a perfectionist; I made some of those mistakes in the beginning. Fortunately I got lucky and hired a guy who had done a lot of rehab work and he was able to guide me through, helping me to not spend time and money on things that weren't going to matter. You have to remember that your standards for rehabbing a house are going to be a lot different than they would be if you were renovating your own house.

Freedom to Live

After I started real estate investing, my wife got really sick and there were probably six months where I didn't do very much at all. I spent very little time on the houses and I remember her saying, "What would I do if you had to go to work? What if you had a job?"

That, to me, that time I was able to spend with her when she was sick was priceless.

I don't know what it would have been like to try to go to work during that time. It's hard to imagine having to get up and go to work when she needed me at home. There were probably six or seven months I spent very little time other than right by her side.

Looking back, I'm sure I did things with my investing business. I might have a two hour window here or there where I could get away and do something. I was able to make calls from the house, things like that. But if I had to be at work by 8 o'clock in the morning and work until I got home at 5 or 6...I know for a fact that I wouldn't have been focusing on my work.

Having that freedom to live my life as I wanted gave me the opportunity to be there for my wife when she needed me. It still allowed me the freedom to come and go, do a little bit here and there, but when it was important that I be home, I was there.

That, truly, is priceless because no amount of money would have made up for that time if I couldn't have been there. That six months was precious time.

I remember reading somewhere that when thinking about being wealthy, it's important to figure out ***why*** you want to be wealthy. It's not enough just to want to be wealthy because you would never get the drive to do it. You have to think about it as more. When I say wealthy, it's more than just the dollar signs.

Wealth is different things to different people.

Who Should Go Into Real Estate Investing

I'm happy to be in real estate investing, and while there is the potential for my kids to go into it, there is nothing that says they **have** to go into it.

Pretty much anyone can do real estate investing, but not everyone is cut out to do it. I'm a firm believer that anyone in the United States can become wealthy.

You have to have the motivation. You have to do it. When I taught the classes for Jim Toner, every one of those people had the same information that I had and even then, out of all the people who actually took the class, a big majority of them never bought a house.

I was a mentor, so when someone picked me out to be their mentor, I bugged them. I called them up and asked, "Have you done this? Have you done that? What are you doing?" I kept pushing them. I only do that for so long, though.

When they don't pick up and run with it...I just don't know. Something's missing and I can't give it to them.

In my case, I see people who go to seminars and get all fired up, but when it comes to doing things they get scared. That's why Jim's program was different. Without the mentorship available, I might not have ever gone anywhere in real estate investing. I'd have doubts and think that it would never work for me.

Now, I'm a big believer in mentorship. That was one of the reasons I took Jim's class. There are a ton of real estate classes out there you can take, and they all have pretty similar information. It's really not rocket science.

But, the one thing that Jim had that the others didn't was the mentorship. When you have questions, as you will, to be able to call someone for help can mean the difference between success and failure.

There are a lot of people out there who might get lucky a time or two, just as I did. But then, they'll make a mistake, and because they didn't have the training or education, they would quit. They would figure, it's just not worth it.

Getting educated and having a mentor will keep you in the game. Without it, it's a crap shoot.

Creating Communities

Almost more than the lifestyle real estate investing offers, I really like the fact that I'm making a difference in my community. That part of this business is really rewarding. When you take a dilapidated eyesore and turn it into a finished project that people walk through and can hardly believe their eyes.

They know how rough it was when I bought it and when they see it after it's been rehabbed, it looks like a totally different place. All those people in the neighborhood know what a difference I've made. And it makes them get "fix it up fever" and they start sprucing up their own homes.

One of the first houses I rehabbed, I bought for $15,000. I rehabbed it and put it back on the market for a great deal more than that. The guy went to get his loan and the bank, who was dealing with my mortgage broker, wanted to see the receipts of what I had put into the house. They couldn't believe the house was worth so much more.

Not only could I provide the receipts, I could send the before and after photos too. I do that with all my houses. I take pictures from the exact same spots before the renovation and then afterward. The minute the bank saw those photos, they stopped asking about the new value of the home.

Soon the bank stopped asking for my receipts. They just wanted to see the before and after pictures. They understood what I was doing and the value I was putting into my properties.

I really love this life. Back when I was engineering, the guys in the shop would all be asking for more and more overtime so that they would take home bigger paychecks.

Overtime was never a goal for me. For me, it was always about lifestyle. The only reason I worked was so I could go home and play. I have tons of hobbies that I do and once I figure out how to make my real estate investing pay me to work on my hobbies I'll consider myself to be a real success.

This life has come really close. I'm the master of my time now.

That is...priceless.

Case Study – Ed Perez

My initial interest in real estate investing came when my wife and I wanted something other than our careers to provide for our financial future. We wanted something that we had some sort of control over. My wife is a nurse and I'm an engineer, and while these are both good jobs, the possibility of suddenly losing one of them always hangs over our heads.

At first we thought about restaurants or a little grocery store attached to a gas station, but we didn't know anything about that. I heard about Jim's seminar one day as I was driving home from work. Fortunately for me, the seminar was being held close by in Cleveland.

I decided to go and hear what Jim Toner had to say about what he's done in the past. When he got to the point where he talked about giving away a free house to a soldier, the coverage was from CNN. That made a big difference to me as far as making a decision. This told me that Jim was legit.

There are so many people out there who just want to take your money.

Before I signed up, though, I had my wife attend the free seminar too. I wanted to make sure that I wasn't just getting caught up in an emotional decision. She came home and said, "Ed, we have to sign up!"

Jim's mentorship program was another big reason we chose to go with him. Once we signed up for the program, we were in it for life. We had mentors, a list of contractors, a list of everything we could possibly need. The mentorship program gave us a one-to-one connection to an assigned mentor. I would call our mentor for any question I had.

When I first started, I knew absolutely nothing about real estate. I relied on their expertise to lead me in the right direction. I signed up in 2008 and four years later I have accumulated fifteen properties. That might sound like a lot, but I still consider myself to still be a novice.

However, for my wife and me, that's a pretty good portfolio. I calculated it to be worth about $875,000 just a little while ago. I concentrated properties in the $80,000 to $110,000 range.

Had I tried to do this without having any direction or having a mentor, I think I would have absolutely failed. Before I learned how to invest in real estate, I would have lost my shirt because I didn't know that the asking price is not always the market value of the property.

Jim's number one rule is, "Make your money when you purchase."

So for me, I want to be between 30% and 60% of the after-repair value. Because I focus on properties between $80,000 and $110,000 a good example would be for a house to sell at $100,000 I want to be able to get it for $30,000 to $60,000, depending on the cost of the rehab. Basically, if the house is on the market for $50,000, I'm not going to buy it right away. I do my math and compare the final number to all the other properties in the area to see if the average price is around $100,000.

Then I have to figure out how much I'm going to be putting into repairs and rehabbing. I make sure that I'm going to make a profit. If I want to get $100,000 out of the property and I can get it for $30,000, I make sure that my rehab costs don't go over $30,000. In that way, I make $40,000 on the deal. This gives you a little room to wiggle if you need to.

We were taught to evaluate everything from the roof all the way down to the basement. From there, if you feel you need to replace the roof, you put the cost of that in the proper place on your sheet. How many squares of shingles do you need...based on the number of shingles, there is a price attached to that.

You just have to write everything down.

Maybe a bathroom needs rehabbing, and it's going to cost about $2,300. Landscaping will cost maybe $1,500. As you go through the property, you put in all the costs of rehabbing. Once you're done, you know what you can offer on the house and wind up making a decent profit.

The very first property I looked at was a foreclosed property. There was so much damage to it I wanted to just walk away from it. We went through the whole property and with that list in our hands they would show us exactly how to do this and what to look for and what types of things to avoid. With Jim's training, the way I looked at properties like that changed.

Dealing with Contractors

You can't get information like that out of a book. Without this kind of training, I would have had contractors taking advantage of me left and right. Let's say the rehab of the property is going to cost $25,000. Many contractors will ask for 50% up front, which translates into $12,500.

That's a lot of money!

I deal with my contractors differently. I hire a contractor and we have a contract that has five deadlines. For the first deadline, I pay the contractor 10%. For the second one, I pay 15%. Then 20%. The very last payment to the contractor is 35%.

The reason I do this is to keep my contractors in check. Some contractors are downright shady once they get your money. They may just run away and you'll never get your money back. You can take them to court, but you will never get your money back.

This way, if a property rehab cost is $25,000 and I pay the contractor the first 10%, that means he has $2,500 to start the demolition on some part of the property.

From there, the next step might be putting in the drywall, and for that I would pay them 15%. As they complete each portion of the project, only then do they get paid.

Now, you're going to have contractors who will try to convince you otherwise, but every time I hire a new contractor, I tell them that I've never worked with them before and I'd be the one on the losing end of the bargain. If they disappear, I'm out the money.

If I decide not to pay them for work they've done, then they know where I live. They can put a lien on my property. The contractors I want to work with understand this logic.

Other contractors will walk away from this arrangement and to me this is just fine. If they don't like the way I structure my payments, they don't have to work with me. Once we're all done, I have the contractor sign an agreement that everything has been paid in full, that I don't owe him any more money and all his subcontractors are paid in full.

This way, his subcontractors can't put a lien on my property.

Before learning all this, I would have just handed over the 50% asking fee and probably been burned. Since I've adopted this approach I've gone through a few contractors. It's all part of the game. Over the past four years I've fired five contractors.

If they're not performing well, they're not showing up, not answering your calls, it means there is something wrong. It means they are trying to hide something from you.

Everything is in my contract agreement. It protects both of us.

Hiring a Good Contractor

Number one rule; don't rely on the business cards they put up at Home Depot. I actually rely on other investors and on my mentor. I'll call my realtors to see if they have someone they would recommend. I also rely on contractors that I use, but who might be busy when I need them. I just ask if there is another contractor who would be willing to work with me.

Another thing I like to do is work with contractors who are in their 50s and 60s. They have been in the business long enough to have developed a good work ethic. I'm a bit leery of a general contractor who is in his 20s or 30s. My experience has been that they aren't always reliable and they often like to party the night before.

I also like to get a guarantee from my contractors. They might say they will get the job done in four weeks. That's great, actually, but I often give them another two weeks. I'll say, "If I give you another two weeks, that's a total of six weeks, can you guarantee that you'll be completely finished?"

Most of the time they agree. Then I insist that we add on a clause where if they go over the six weeks they have to pay me $100 for every day they go over the agreed upon time frame. Now they know that they better not take this job and then take on another one in the meantime, making me wait for a few extra weeks. They better get the work done on my property otherwise it is going to start costing them some money.

That's one of the best methods I use for keeping my contractors coming every day and getting done what they promise.

Mentorship

I feel absolutely great knowing that I have Jim and all his people at my disposal. I know that I have somebody behind me if I run into problems. I'm still a novice and I haven't experienced everything that can go wrong in the real estate business.

I had to evict some tenants, and I wouldn't have known how to go about doing that if I weren't given the proper guidance. A lot of people are afraid of becoming landlords with tenants because they don't know how to get rid of them if they become problems. In the state of Ohio, there is a process you have to use. Many states have a very specific process on how you can evict people.

Once you follow the process, then you go in and change the locks. Having your "rent due" and "eviction notice" in your contract helps a lot. Say your rent is due on the first of the month, and by the third of the month you haven't received any money. We will post a three day eviction notice. After three days, we through the court and apply to file for eviction.

It is a fairly smooth process. Before I understood this, I thought it was a pretty complicated process. The negative aspect to evicting tenants is that they often do damage to your property. But, this is part of this business.

Without having the education and mentorship on learning how to evict non-paying tenants, I wouldn't have been comfortable at all in booting out people who won't pay their rent. I have repeatedly called my mentors and gotten the perfect guidance every time, and I learn a little better each time how to communicate with my tenants.

The Benefits of Being a Real Estate Investor

I really like what I do. I've finally found something that I really enjoy doing. I *really like* being a real estate investor. I like it because I work so many hours a month but at the end of the month I get a nice big paycheck. Because I'm a one-man operation, I don't have a property management company, I work my business about eight to nine hours a month. That works out to about two hours a week.

Most of my tenants are absolutely wonderful. We see eye-to-eye on things, and we both honor our side of our agreements. As a result, I get calls from other people I've never met wanting to rent from me because they have heard how well I treat my tenants. I send them Christmas cards, Birthday cards, and once a year I would select one of my tenants as the "Best Tenant of the Year" and they would get one month's free rent.

Let me tell you, they *love* it when they get a letter that says, "Congratulations, you have just won the Best Tenant of the Year Award. You will receive one month's stay rent-free because of your good standing with us."

Support from Friends and Family

When I first got started in real estate investing, my coworkers all tried to talk me out of it. They told me all kinds of horror stories about how I would have to evict all my tenants, that they would trash my properties, and current property values are so depressed that I would just be wasting my money.

After I did a couple of renovations, I brought in pictures so that they could see the before and after photos. Now they really are impressed with what I've been able to do.

My biggest piece of advice came from this experience of getting advice from all my coworkers and friends. None of them were landlords, and yet they were full of all kinds of advice for me and how I should or shouldn't run my real estate investing business. They would ask me why I was putting my money in real estate, and then tell me things like:

"The market is falling."

"Why are you investing now? You'll lose money."

They don't know what they are talking about. Interestingly enough, now, when questions arise at work about finance and investing, they now turn to me.

So, for those who are reading this book be careful about taking advice from people who have never done what you're planning to do. Get a mentor who **knows** the business and get your advice there.

As far as my family is concerned, they have been very supportive of my efforts. In fact, they like to invest with me as well, so I use their money instead of from hard money lenders.

My family listened to me. I would tell them that if they have their money in a savings account or a CD they would be making between less than 1% up to 3%. If they let me invest their money, I can give them a 10% return on their investment per year. It's a safe investment and this is a really great way to get money to invest in this business.

You need to have a little bit of money. I know some people out there say you don't, but you really do need to have some money to get started. Because of this financial support from my family, I've been able to not only help myself, but my family as well.

The really great thing is that I love real estate. Every time I go to a website, it's about real estate. I check out websites that talk about what is going on in my area. I hope, one day, to be linked with Jim Toner or some of the other people who really know what they're talking about in terms of real estate. These are the kind of mentors you should find when you get into real estate, and one day, I plan to be one of them too. I've been in this business for about four years and I now have fifteen properties.

Now, I will say, real estate investing is not for everyone. People may not like dealing with tenants, or with contractors. In my opinion, it takes a certain kind of person to be successful in real estate investing. You have to have a bit of an entrepreneurial mindset in order to be successful.

Section 8 Housing

Speaking of dealing with tenants, one thing I hear from some people is that they worry about getting Section 8 housing tenants. Perhaps hearing my experiences will help to put your fears to rest.

Personally, my experience is that more renters who are *not* Section 8 give me excuses for not coming up with the rent.

"I was sick."

"I ran out of gas."

"My mother's sick."

"I haven't gone to the bank this week so I don't have the money for you."

With Section 8, I've noticed that they will do everything right away because they are very grateful to have such a great place to rent and they don't want to jeopardize it.

If they violate the contract of Section 8, they're out of the program. I think here in Ohio, they're out of the program for four years. They don't want to mess it up for their family, so they are much more responsible about taking care of their housing.

Also, when they move from one property to another, say they had another kid or something; they leave your property spotless. That's not to say there aren't some bad apples, because there are. But for the most part, my renters who are Section 8 qualified will do everything possible to keep me happy.

Everyone wants/needs good housing. It doesn't matter if you're down on your luck or not. These people need a home and I treat all my renters as equals unless they give me a reason to think otherwise. Most of my renters are like friends to me.

Unfortunately, a few of my non-Section 8 renters haven't been as good. When they keep coming up with excuses, I pretty much draw the line and don't let things drag on for too long. Obviously, if they've been a good tenant for a long time and then experience some financial difficulties, I'll work with them.

When I see this behavior becoming a pattern, I am less likely to work with them. I'm nice, but I'm not a pushover. Sadly, if you're a nice person, some people will see that as a weakness.

Mentorship

If I hadn't been involved with Jim's course and the mentorship program that he developed, I think I would still be stuck back in my old lifestyle.

This is what I see with people who just talk about getting involved in real estate investing. They start talking about it, then a year goes by, five years go by, a decade goes by and they're still sitting there and "talking" about it.

For me, once I came across Jim Toner's program I was very satisfied that it would give me the information and guidance I needed to make a change in my life.

I understand how other people may not be convinced that real estate investing is the way to financial security. That's OK for them. For me, this is the only way to go, but I wouldn't do it without having someone I can call whenever I have a question.

Without a doubt, having a mentor means the difference between being successful and failing. You don't have to be very smart to be successful in real estate. I'm a really good engineer and did well in school. But just because I'm a good engineer doesn't mean I knew everything there is to know about real estate investing.

What I'm really happy about is my kids are viewing real estate as a way to financial security. My oldest wants to be an orthodontist, but she also wants to get into real estate investing when she gets older.

All my kids enjoy picking up a hammer and helping with some of the demolition work. They see what I do, they pay attention, and it gives them a little idea of how it feels to be in the real estate business. They really enjoy it.

One of my coworkers was interested in real estate investing. She had taken a seminar years ago from a really famous guy, but it didn't pan out for her. There was no guidance and no mentorship. I told her about Jim Toner's seminar, and after she attended the seminar, she signed up for the program. Now she's happy too.

Money, Where to Get It

Before anyone gets into real estate investing, it's a good idea to take of your other debt before you get involved. I know some people get into real estate investing to get *rid* of their debt, and it might work for them.

The way I did it is I had about $70,000 in savings. I build my house back in 2002 and after eight years my property was worth $375,000 and I only owed $98,000 on it. I was really pouring money into paying this house off. But the best thing I ever did was take out equity from that house because the equity was earning me zero dollars! When I took out that home equity loan, that's what I used to finance my other properties and they are now making me money.

My oldest properties are large enough and doing well enough that my bank says, "Ed, you can start your own company. You don't have to put your name as the borrower. You can use your company name as the borrower. I'm glad I am able to borrow money using my company.

Jim taught us to have our own LLC, which I did. I'm glad I did that because if anyone were ever to sue me, it would be limited to my LLC as opposed to being sued personally. That's the best thing I ever did.

The other place I get money is from my family. I borrowed money from people around me because money is there. I explained what I was doing to my brother-in-law and he wanted to get into real estate investing too. He's helping me out financially speaking.

My mother-in-law gave me $70,000 and she gets a 10% return on that; which is $7,000 a year. That's a really good return on your money.

My parents also invested and are very happy with their return on their money. To them, it is an excellent way to subsidize their retirement income.

People ask me what I'm going to do when I retire. I'm only 46 now and I work for the EPA in Ohio. I have only seven years to go before I reach my 30th year with them. At that point, I can retire from the EPA, but I don't believe I will *ever* retire from real estate investing.

Circle of Experts

In addition to mentorship, the other thing you have to build around you in real estate investing is your circle of experts. You'll need an attorney, a real estate agent, a property manager, and contractors.

You will want to develop this circle of experts carefully. It's a smart move to surround yourself with smart people. I can never be an attorney. I don't want to be a realtor. So, finding the best people around is how I surround myself with great expertise that I don't have to possess myself.

The best way to find good people is talking to other people. Ask questions, who do they know? Who's good? Get background information, and keep digging until you're satisfied.

This is where having that mentorship comes in handy. I would call up Jim Toner and ask him what other things I should ask of these various people. Jim and my other investor friends would give me suggestions. I knew I could trust these people, and as a result in only four years I have fifteen properties making over six figures a year.

Five years ago, I never would have believed I would be making six figures as a real estate investor. My wife and I were making decent money at that time. But now I'm making more money with a lot less effort.

I'll admit, in the beginning, it took more effort than it does now. I was learning how to deal with contractors, deal with the various kinds of tenants and things like that. Once tenants are established in the property, the business pretty much runs itself. I spend about eight to ten hours a month on my business.

I also have good contractors that I work with regularly too. When I have a new property, I know I have a good guy to go to.

That's a really good thing for people to know, once you find a really good contractor, you never let him go! I never even give out this guy's name. It's like I don't want to share my girlfriend with another guy! I want my contractor for myself.

For smaller jobs, I have a number of handymen I call. If I need a faucet fixed, a dishwasher installed, or something, I use one of those guys. As far as this goes, I also like to find guys in their 50's or 60's. Generally speaking, they have a better work ethic. If they are young and have a brand new shiny truck, I'm a little skeptical. The older guys with the well-used truck, they've been at this business for a long time.

Final Words of Advice

Do your homework. Get a little background information. Learn what you can about the business.

I know you've probably heard this over and over, but if I can do it, anyone can do it. You just have to put your mind to it.

Actually, put your mind to *you*. What do *you* want?

At first, I wasn't really much of one for reading books. Now I read books all the time on real estate. Once I got really excited about real estate investing, I now read everything I can get my hands on.

Set some rules in the beginning. One other thing I do when I look at a property is determine what my capitalization rate will be, how many years will it be before I get my money back.

If I can expect to get my money back in eight or nine years, that's a good investment. If it is going to take fifteen to twenty years, I walk away from the opportunity. That just a rule of thumb I use. Other people don't mind waiting longer for their return. This is one way I can quickly make decisions about a property.

For those of you who think you want to get into real estate investing because you've bought your own home, maybe a couple of times, investment real estate is a different animal. When you look for a home you plan to live in, you're looking for something that is ready to go, top notch. You don't necessarily want to do a lot of work in terms of renovation.

Because you're going to be living in it, you're looking for a home, not an investment.

My investment properties always get new paint, countertops, cabinets, etc. but it's different than preparing a home for your family. I turn a bad property around and it will become a home for someone who is looking for something like that.

I know a woman who decided to get into real estate investing thinking she knew everything she needed. She asked me for some advice and I gave it to her. But because she was looking at the house as if it were going to be her home, she did a lot of upgrades she really shouldn't have done. She also hired a contractor without getting a contract. I warned her against that, but she didn't listen. She got hosed because she didn't have any mentors. Sure, she was asking me questions, but she wasn't listening to my answers.

If you get a real estate investing mentor, make sure you listen to them and follow their advice. There's no point in paying someone for their mentorship, and then ignoring their advice. You may not want to do what they say, but it's usually in your best interest to. It's kind of like when your Mom and Dad say you should or shouldn't do something. You don't like hearing it, but they're usually right.

Do your homework, do your research, and when you get a mentor...make sure you listen!

Case Study – Dave and Irina

Dave – In the Beginning

We're a husband and wife real estate investing team working together on our business.

Before learning anything about real estate investing, we bought a property, a duplex next door to the house that we owned. The owner was an absentee landlord and over the years there were a number of undesirables living there. When I saw the property go up for sale, I bought the property.

I'll admit that I had no idea what I was doing. After purchasing the property, I spent about six months refurbing the property. This goes against all the advice you've been given, but I hadn't been trained in real estate investing yet. Actually, I enjoyed doing the work, but it definitely consumed all of my time.

The deal worked out well for me. I was able to rent out the duplex and saw that there was something to this real estate investing game. We bought another property, did all the rehab, working for about a year on that property. Both Irina and I worked full time, so the rehab work was eating up all our spare time. Pretty much every available moment for a year was spent getting that place ready to rent.

It was after we had finished this second property that we heard of Jim Toner's free seminar. That was about seven or eight years ago now. The seminar presented a plan that sounded like it might be easier than what we had been doing, completing all the work ourselves. Apparently this is a common problem with untrained real estate investors.

Because we were intrigued by what we learned at his free seminar, we made an appointment to meet with Jim. I'll freely admit that we were skeptical.

There are so many real estate investing programs out there, and we all know that a bunch of them are scams. We went into our meeting with Jim feeling a little gun-shy, not because of anything I'd experienced myself, it is just my nature. Although, most people will tell you of all the horror stories they've heard about getting into real estate investing, so I've heard my share of them.

Irina, on the other hand, had the advantage of not hearing those kinds of prejudicial horror stories, so she was on board a lot faster than I was. I was thinking that we did a pretty good job on the deals we had already done. I've never been afraid of taking a chance; I just want to know what I'm getting into. While I may have gone about it the wrong way, I was still somewhat successful.

Anyone who considers going into real estate investing will meet a ton of people who will try to talk you out of it. Probably ninety percent of the people who go to the seminar will never actually start investing in real estate.

They will allow the negative opinions of other people to prevent them from doing it.

Actually, I got roped into a few scams, so I met with Jim with a very healthy dose of skepticism. I've been able to read people pretty well, and I trust my gut. Our conversation with Jim put me at ease very quickly. We talked about our philosophies of life and we just meshed.

Irina had made up her mind that we would participate, while I went to the interview not thinking I was going to become a member of his organization.

We spent an hour just talking with Jim, chatting about life experiences and we developed a real level of comfort talking with him. We had similar backgrounds. Neither Jim nor I had the benefit of a college education.

Obviously from talking to Jim, he was a successful real estate investor. But even more important than that was Jim's involvement with various charities. It's important to Jim to share what he earns and that something that really resonated with us because we feel the same way.

Our friendship grew, not really because of the real estate investing side of things, but from the charities we were involved with. He was involved with some of the same charities, so that told us he was a good guy.

We decided to take his course and take advantage of his mentorship program. Jim's seminar talks about getting out of your job and getting into real estate investing full time. That's not what Irina and I were looking for.

We were looking for a way to build our long-term retirement program and maybe retire a little earlier than what was in the cards for us. I think what really appealed to us was that Jim's system could be adapted to work with the different goals that we had in mind.

Our initial goal was to build up a better retirement plan than the average 401K and maybe retire a little earlier. With that goal in mind, we took the course that Jim offered. Jim's mentorship program was also something that was different from other programs that we had looked into.

Many of the other programs out there have you do some book learning or classroom training and then you are left to your own devices to go out and do it. The mentorship and coaching program really set Jim apart.

We started this real estate investing as a part-time side business. Since starting, we now have twenty properties that we bought, rehabbed, and still own.

We have done a couple of flips using his methods and even got into some side things where we have been able to help people out with short-term loans that have worked out well for both parties involved.

For Irina and me, real estate investing gives us something to work on together and it helps us to get closer to one another.

Irina – In the Beginning

Unlike Dave, I didn't have much experience with real estate. I grew up in Moscow where real estate ownership is nothing like it is in the U.S. I agreed to become involved because this is something Dave wanted to do.

I didn't expect to get as interested in real estate investing as I did, and I now do more of the daily work of the business than Dave. In fact, my interest was so great that I actually got my real estate license.

When I came to the United States, I was in a good situation because I owned a business in Russia and I could continue working for my business in Russia online from here. The business was about construction materials. When I was in Russia, it was my full-time job, but here it was only part-time because I'm limited by the things that I can do online. My partner in Russia takes care of the rest of the business.

I had just met Dave and we began dating. Initially we were not thinking about getting married or anything, but we did not live far from each other. I lived in a duplex that I rented, and was very happy that the other side of the duplex was vacant. I didn't want neighbors next door.

One day, I saw a For Sale sign in the yard and it alarmed me. The reason it bothered me is that the duplex had only one shared driveway and I was the one using it. I feared that when the duplex sold, someone else would move in and they would want to use the driveway. To me, it was a disaster! I know that's a little funny, but it was the way my mind was thinking.

I asked Dave, "What would you suggest I do?"

Dave said, "Why don't you buy it?"

So, that's what I did. I wasn't thinking about getting into real estate investing. I'm just the kind of person who would regret what I do rather than regret what I don't do. So, I just did it.

Dave already had his rental property, and we talked about the numbers and everything made sense to me. I just took it from there. From that experience I learned that business is business, no matter what you do. It could be running a construction materials business online or it can be a real estate investing business. You just do what you need to do.

When I decided to get involved in real estate, I decided to just jump into it. I knew I had to learn what I was doing. Fortunately, I didn't have a language problem. I took whatever courses I could. And, of course, Dave was always there when I didn't understand something and I asked thousands of questions!

It was after I bought the duplex that we decided we should probably set up a company and be professional about how we ran our real estate investing business. Right after that is when we went to Jim Toner's real estate investing course and naturally we took the course together.

Taking that course really changed how Dave saw this business. At first I think he looked at real estate as a hobby that we enjoyed dabbling in. After taking Jim's course he started changing how he looked at it, and I already saw it as a business. Dave realized we were partners in this business, and it was no longer a hobby.

He says I keep him grounded in how we approach our real estate investing business.

Dave – The Birth of a Business

When Irina says I looked at the business as a hobby, it was because I really enjoyed working on properties. Because I enjoyed the work, I didn't really think too much about the final numbers when I considered buying a property.

It never occurred to me that while I was working on a place for a whole year, that if I had hired a contractor instead, it would have been done in two or three weeks. I could have collected eleven months' worth of rent.

Instead, the time I was working on the property, I had it tied up **not** making me money. Sure, it would cost me more to have that contractor working on it, but once the place was done, the money would start coming in. Positive cash flow is always a good thing.

That was a wakeup call for me. The good thing is that even when I was looking at it as a hobby, we did pretty well on those first couple of properties. Our **wrong** system still made us money. But we did give up a lot of personal time. Jim showed us that there was a better way of doing this business.

Some people, like us, get into real estate investing and make this mistake. They buy a property, then spend all their spare time doing all the work to refurb it. After doing this a couple of times, they get burned out and don't want to do real estate investing. And when you do it this way, it **is** a lot of work!

In addition to all that work, you're paying utilities, taxes, and mortgage on a property that isn't earning you money. Once you have tenants in there, those are all taken care of.

Also, when you can start churning out your properties like this, we can set business goals. Our goal is to not stop at just one property, but the instant a property is refurbed and rented, we're looking for our next property in a month or two. My old way of doing things, I was only doing one property a year. It takes a very long time to build up our retirement account doing it that way.

With this new method, we can do five or six properties in a year rather than just one. The beauty is that we're doing this business part-time. We pick and choose which properties we want to handle.

Last year, we had a lot of family issues we had to address and work out. Some of them are ongoing, but because we can scale back our business when we want to, we can handle things at our own pace and get through these personal issues and we still have our existing properties making money for us.

We're moving toward a phase where we can begin to be more active in our acquisitions again, and that's exciting. Our typical approach is to take one day out of a weekend a month to look for properties. This would be actually going to the properties and physically looking at them. We've already done our research online.

Because Irina has a Real Estate license, she has access to the MLAs and can do a lot of things that the average investor can't do.

We also do things that Jim doesn't necessarily advise; we like to acquire our properties in different ways. We bought several off of Craigslist, and we bought a property from HUD. We like gaining as much knowledge as possible.

Typically, Irina would do a little bit of looking ahead of time. I would spend an evening or two a week looking on Craigslist and making phone calls. I'd talk to the sellers to see if a property we were interested in would be worth looking at. In this way, we weed out a lot of properties that we probably wouldn't be interested in.

There would also be times when Irina would go and check out properties without me and would eliminate the ones that I knew definitely did not fit the property profile we were looking for.

On that Saturday or Sunday, we might have about a dozen properties we would to and physically look at. We would decide what we thought needed to be done to the properties, and once we got home we would crunch the numbers on the estimated repair costs. You figure in the anticipated rents, plug everything into the formula and we would then decide if we wanted to make an offer.

We limit ourselves to one property at a time, so once an offer has been accepted, we work that property until it is refurbed and rented. You certainly don't have to do that, but for us, it helped to preserve our sanity. We have done three or four projects at the same time, and we decided that was just too stressful. We backed off that idea pretty quickly.

We are probably more willing to buy places that need more work than a lot of other beginning real estate investing students. I'm a lot more comfortable with it because I've done a lot of the work myself, so I know what to expect.

The average house would take about a month to acquire, then another month to rehab. Once the properties are ready, we usually rent them very quickly. Once a property is done, we're ready to look for the next project, so we will put financing on the completed property and purchase the next one. It's a process that we repeat over and over.

Getting Tenants Quickly

There are probably three pieces to our formula for getting tenants quickly:

1. Make your property nicer than your competition. At the very least, make the property as nice as possible compared to its competition in the same neighborhood. We like to feel we rent very nice properties. Our company motto is, "Nice homes for nice people." Our homes are spotlessly clean. Irina sometimes thinks I'm too much of a fanatic about this, but I usually do the final cleaning before we start showing the property.
2. Price the property competitively.
3. Advertise where people look. About 80% of our properties are rented off of Craigslist. We take pictures, write up an enticing ad, post it with our phone number and wait for the phone to ring. Or, they will email us and we give them more information about the property.

Once we have done this, we do what we can to get multiple appointments at around the same time and we try to get them to fill out an application when they come to view the property. We space the appointments about fifteen minutes apart because we don't want to waste our time. You'll have some no-shows, and then other people are chronically late. By having numerous people coming within an hour's time, you're not wasting your time.

There is also the added benefit that when people see that there is other interest in the property, it can help them to make a decision about leasing right away.

Irina – Advantages of Being a Real Estate Agent

The main advantage for us is that I can do my own research when I want to. I don't have to wait for another Realtor to do the research and get it to me. I can also just jump in the car and go look at the properties without making an appointment with a Realtor.

Not only does it save us a lot of time, but I can choose better because I know exactly what we're looking for. I hate to see them wasting their time when I can do a lot of this myself and on our own time. I feel more comfortable doing much of these things myself.

You see, many Realtors don't really understand what investors are looking for. Most agents just aren't in tune with that. The real estate investor is unique and we have different things we're looking for. Most agents know how to sell a property to someone who just buys a house to live in.

As a result, they focus only on properties that are "move-in" ready. They know the right things to say to motivate those types of buyers, they talk about how cute the yard is, or how to envision us sitting in the living room. It always drove Dave nuts when we would walk into a kitchen and the realtor would say, "Here's the kitchen." Dave's already opening up the cabinet underneath the sink to see what kind of faucet valves are under there.

We don't need to be told those kinds of things. We want to know what needs to be fixed and what kind of rent we can expect once we're finished. Before I became a Realtor, we had to endure them telling us how our dining room table would look in this or that corner.

It's not their fault. That's how they're trained to present a property. And because they just didn't understand the mentality of an investor, they would give us a list of maybe twenty properties and only one or two might fit our needs. We wasted a lot of time looking at properties that we would have ruled out if we just had a little more information.

The other problem with agents working with real estate investors is the commission is so small. Investors are looking for a deal, and it is almost not worth an agent's time for what then end up getting from the sale of that property. It's too hard for them to make a living when they deal exclusively with investors.

The last thing that convinced us that I should get my real estate license is the properties we were interested in, they might have utilities turned off, or there might be inspection issues, zoning issues, etc. Your average agent doesn't know how to deal with those things. We ended up doing all this kind of legwork anyway because if we didn't things didn't work out as smoothly.

Marketing for Tenants/Buyers

When we sell houses, we do a very nice lead-in on the internet, like a short story. We put all the pictures together into a moving slideshow. Because we do extra on our marketing like the videos, our results are really great.

Through Jim, we got to know Frank McKinney. Now, he's a real estate investor who is probably the best in the world. He has given us some coaching on how to do videos like this. We take everything to heart, take the extra step, put in the extra effort, and all this puts us a notch above our competition. The videos we use are hosted by YouTube. The home page shows the properties we have for sale, and when you click on the picture, it takes you to the video that showcases the property.

Fortunately, we took Frank's advice and put it to use very quickly. I can't say that I have always done that with Jim's advice. Irina will tell you I'm a little bit of a slow learner that way and probably should have taken Jim's advice a lot sooner.

Many new real estate investors suffer from this same problem. I tend to do something myself, fail, and then go and get help. Or, I might not fail, but realize that there might be an easier, simpler, or less expensive way to go about doing something.

Surrounding yourself with experts is the way to go. Irina got her Real Estate license, so she's my first expert there. Jim's our mentor, another expert there. Frank McKinney has also been very generous with his coaching as well. The key for a new real estate investor to learn is that you don't have to be an expert in everything involved in the process in order to be successful.

Handling Fear

A lot of people don't go into real estate investing because they're afraid. There is a lot of fear involved, and if you don't get some education about hit, find experts and mentors, you can come up with probably a million reasons why you shouldn't get into real estate investing.

The key is eliminating that fear. If you allow even one fear to control you, you will fail. Guaranteed. If you don't believe you can be successful, you will fail, and that's what it amounts to.

The biggest fear people have is dealing with tenants. Another one is fear of the unknown in the purchase...most people just don't know what to expect unless they've gotten some education in this area.

Then, there is the fear of losses. People think, "What happens when I sign that paper on closing day for a deal that might be more than my net worth?" That's a scary proposition.

You just have to get up and start doing. If you just move past all those fears and reasons and focus on your motivating factor, you can be a success at this business.

Working as a Team

Our biggest advantage is that Irina and I work together as a team. We know some other husband and wife teams, but usually one is more involved than the other. In our business model, we're both fully involved, and because we work together on this business, it has brought us closer because it is just one more thing that we have in common.

We really enjoy working together toward a common goal. We are building up a nice retirement down the road at the end, but the biggest side benefit for us is the fact that it has allowed us to be a lot more generous in our charities.

Philanthropic Activities

Being able to help others is definitely one of the driving goals for both of us. We have already mentioned that Frank McKinney has given us some suggestions in how we can improve our business. But, more importantly, we are really happy to be involved with Frank's charitable foundation, Caring House in Haiti.

We have been to Haiti multiple times and this would have never happened without the extra revenue we have generated as a result of our real estate dealings.

Charitable work is really my driving passion behind all of this. Real estate is a nice way to generate revenue and maybe provide a little better life for both of us. We had a little extra money, bolstered our retirement accounts and maybe bought a couple extra toys.

But, then you move beyond that phase. This life we live isn't just about us.

Being able to get involved in the charities and being able to make bigger donations than we were ever able to do from our day jobs. That is a really moving experience. We make enough money to get by with our day jobs. It's plenty to pay our bills and daily living expenses.

The real estate and all the extra revenue that generates is our model now. We don't live off the money we make from our real estate investing. Half of that money we reinvest into the business, the other half we donate to various charities.

You'll talk to a lot of real estate investors who make friends with other investors. And we have done that. But even better, we've made some amazing like-minded friends through our charitable activities; it is these friends who have become very close to us.

This is what drives us.

Different people are motivated by different things. I've worked with Jim, speaking to some of his groups and over the years I've noticed that the majority of the people are motivated by the idea of more money for toys or to pay off bills, things like that. But some are motivated by being able to provide for themselves, their family, and others.

Interestingly enough, these are the people who wind up being more successful over the years.

So, in the end, get over your fear. Believe in what you're doing. Focus on something bigger than yourself, and don't let a single bad experience chase you away. We learn from our failures, and won't make the same mistake twice. Whether it is dealing with inept contractors or tenants who are less desirable than you would want, every experience teaches you something.

Case Study – Evan Mendenhall

I have been called a young entrepreneur. I'm twenty-four, and to some people that might seem young. My journey to real estate investing wasn't my initial foray into the entrepreneurial lifestyle. In the beginning I wanted to do something with animals. I hadn't really fleshed out this idea, so I wasn't sure how I would accomplish this.

What I started to notice is that I found that no matter what I tended to do, I would find ways to make money in my pocket.

I went to Hawaii once, I was twelve years-old, and I left the Islands with $400 in my pocket because I helped some local people find out something they needed. I guess I've always had that entrepreneurial drive; figuring out ways to provide a service to make money.

When I was around sixteen I heard Jim Toner's radio advertisement and I told my mom that she should probably go and see how it goes and try to learn about real estate. I was still in high school, working in produce and sort of excluded myself from the opportunity. She went and learned a little about it, but didn't end up getting any properties. I continued working in produce for a couple of years and started going to college. One day, in produce, I remember it exactly, I was putting two red peppers on the table and I said, "I've got to find a way to make more money than two hundred dollars a week!"

I came up with six different business ideas. One of my close friends, a stock options trader, was in his 40s. He told me that all these ideas would probably work, but if I really wanted to make money, there was an opportunity the he knew of. He was the software designer of a retail sales company, traveled across the country selling pet supplies. Because of my interest in animals, I got in contact with this company. I went to work for them, and dropped out of college after doing three semesters. The president of this company is a super entrepreneur who basically builds companies and then sells them. He said that he would mentor me if I would read these books....so I started learning from a mega-entrepreneur and he told me I needed to find passive investment.

As I started to build up money in this sales company, I remembered I needed to learn that I had to get the assets to pay me. I remembered Jim Toner. I bought his course full out. I paid the full price and said, "I know if Jim Toner is successful in doing this, then he can teach me. If anyone can do it, then anyone else can do it too as long as they model it appropriately."

What I tried to do, basically, is follow Jim Toner's program to the letter. It worked for me. Now I have properties that are producing income. That's pretty much where I am right now.

My First Purchase

Getting into real estate investing never really bothered me. I know a lot of people have a lot of fears and concerns about getting involved it, but I just didn't go there. What I figured was that I would never get anywhere just sitting on my couch.

My plan was to work long enough to make a down payment, but I ended up putting money into Jim's course. I listened to his Quick Start audio and learned how important it was to take action. You have to be brave.

"OK," I said to myself, "I'm going to do that."

His course taught me how to contact and find real estate agents. I found one, Gary Wilson, of all people, good friends of Jim Toner. Within two days, Gary Wilson took me out and showed me some properties. I said, "OK, let's look at these numbers. You have the experience. What makes the most sense?"

He said, "This is producing this amount and it costs this much."

I said, "Ok, let's do it." Within two or three days from starting this course, I got hooked up with a real estate agent and I started the process on the first house.

I didn't go into this with any kind of rehab design in mind. I wanted what is called a "turnkey" investment. This was a triplex that had tenants in it already and it was producing income. I looked at the mortgage payment and the taxes and insurance, it came to a little over four hundred dollars. The rental income was fourteen hundred dollars. I thought, "OK, this makes sense." I looked at the repairs that needed to be done and we went through the normal worksheet that Jim gave us.

From there I actually did a mail away closing while I was off on vacation. It was interesting. I was in Hawaii at the time. I finished closing on the property, and I only saw it once, made the decision, and from there it started to make income.

Jim was personally there every step of the way when I had questions: What should I look for on this type of a house…it wasn't covered in his audio, which most things were. Then, I literally would just call up his office and he would tell me. I didn't know anything about what I should look for in terms of the condition of the house. I didn't know if it was bad, if the roof was in shambles, or if the walls were…I just didn't know. So…in working with the realtor, he helped out by showing what needed to be fixed, what I could overlook for now, and when he said it was a good income producing property, so I jumped ahead and bit the bullet.

Becoming a landlord was certainly a new experience, but for me that was one of the most fun parts about this life. It was certainly worth the risk and the learning curve of having something, owning something that makes money. Your money works for you rather than you working for money.

The shift I wanted to make as soon as I could. Even if it didn't work out, whatever I learned from the failure would help me make it work the next time. I wasn't so much afraid as excited to get going.

To people who are afraid of becoming a landlord I would say, "Life is just about the passion. Just go for it!" There is so much to learn. Failure won't kill you. But failure to change might.

It was either Zig Ziglar or Tony Robbins who said, "Success leaves clues. The people who are achieving everything in life, the money, the family, the relationships, they have pretty much have laid the path. There is no need to be afraid. It's like following a recipe, if you're making a cake in the kitchen, you use a recipe and you make a cake."

The key is you find the people who are living the way you want, do the things that they do, and your life will end up being very similar. It is very important to choose well and fortunately, I had a lot of great people in my life who were living the way I wanted to live, and Jim Toner was one of them. He said to put your fear aside and I did and it worked out.

I was twenty when I left college, having completed three semesters of business administration. I realized that business was not going to make me money. I should be following the people who are making money today and see what they're doing.

My mentor, who initially took me under his wing, suggested I read books to improve my mind. Here are a few of the books I read to get me ready for the entrepreneurial life:

- *Think and Grow Rich* – Napoleon Hill
- *The Richest Man in Babylon* – George S. Clason
- *The Greatest Salesman in the World* – Og Mandino
- *Launching a Leadership Revolution* – Chris Brady
- *How to Win Friends and Influence People* – Dale Carnegie
- *The Richest Man Who Ever Lived* – Steven K. Scott

Be an Individual

None of my friends were doing what I was doing at all. I have always been the guy to go against the grain, which is what Frank McKinney tells us," Be a Maverick."

When I left college to do sales, travel across the country, I had a good solid group of about twelve high school friends who hung out every Friday and Saturday. It was great. But when I shared my plans, they all thought I was completely crazy. They were very outspoken about their opinions. They thought I was throwing my life away by leaving college and going into sales.

I knew I needed to make money and I needed to learn to sell so I could eventually build companies and start building real estate and things like that.

Everyone thought I was crazy. I was the only one doing it. But, I looked outside my group of friends for support.

One of my favorite things about reading is that it puts you in touch with the minds of great men that you wouldn't otherwise meet. Through reading and through audio, you can really get the support and the close mentorship, even without meeting anyone. They can help you build the confidence you need to take more steps when your friends are just not having your back.

Reading books and listening to audios made all the difference for me. I try to listen to or read something positive every single day. What that will do is stimulate my mind to think in a new way. Even if I have heard an audio say forty or fifty times, I believe you just can't hear the fundamentals enough.

The fundamentals, the basics of success, they're just very practical and I love hearing them because it keys my brain to a higher vibration. Listening to audios or reading a book just fills my mind with possibilities. It shows me what other people have done.

The success of other people excites me. I believe that I can certainly do what they have done, or what I have set my mind to doing. Then, I know that I can share and teach other people how to do this. They can live the life they want to live.

Every single day, I listen to something positive or I'll read one of these books. I love doing this.

What Makes Me Different

There are tons of seminars out there, and I know that a lot of people go to them, get all hyped up but as soon as they come home, they put the binders and tapes up on the shelf and say, "I'll get to it later." That kind of approach isn't going to do a thing for you.

There really is very little difference between me and someone who goes to a seminar and then procrastinates upon their return. The difference, really, is miniscule. It's that I'll take a single step.

Taking that first step is all it takes. If you can just get past the first feeling of resistance you have, your first action will create energy and as soon as you take action you didn't want to take, you become motivated.

Motivation literally follows the action. I have learned that whenever I don't want to do something, I'll want to procrastinate. As soon as I notice myself procrastinating, I know that is the perfect opportunity for me to grow as a person.

Because I want to grow as a person, I'll take that action, no matter how small it is...even when I don't want. Especially if I don't want to!

Just like everyone else, I procrastinate, but as soon as I notice that's what I'm doing, I just start doing something. Once I get into activity, I literally become motivated to get it done. I'm now excited. Motivation creates energy to keep going. I've personally experienced this and I know it works.

I'm just like all the knowledge junkies out there who love the seminars and the books. The only difference is my ability to take that initial action, which is just as hard for me as it is for anyone else.

But, everyone can do it. That's the thing! That's the secret!

When you give in to procrastination, it becomes a bigger problem every day you ignore it. I've had a problem with procrastination too. I've just learned to put positive leverage on myself. We always do what we want to do, no matter what that is. In order to achieve the results I want out of life I have to convince myself that it is worth it.

People want to quit smoking, but when they look at a cigarette, they would rather have the feeling of smoking right now than the long-term effect of being off cigarettes.

You have to ask yourself, "Do I want to live the way I'm envisioning, or do I want to watch this TV show?"

I make a list of reasons I want to do something, and then I'll check them off. When I procrastinate, I do it fully aware that I'm choosing to procrastinating, that I'm putting off doing something that I should be doing.

Finding a way to motivate myself is very, very important. I have to be able to do this; otherwise, I'd never get anything done. I learned a lot about motivating people when I was in charge of leading sales teams across the country. It has everything to do with the person motivating themselves. Everyone has their own way of doing it, they get themselves into an excited space and when the emotion is hot, the idea is strong, that is the time to act.

It is so much better to just take that action; otherwise, as Jim Rohn said, "It becomes the law of diminishing intent." We all intend to do it when the idea strikes us, but we sometimes allow it to be swept away.

If I were to go back to my group of twelve friends I used to hand out with on Friday and Saturday nights, I would have some very different things to say to them. I would say, "Listen guys, if you do exactly what I did, you could be exactly where I am." I think they could all do it, with maybe a couple of exceptions...I don't have a family, and that really could make what I'm doing a lot harder. Most families don't want a parent traveling most of the time.

But, if they could have a definite picture in mind, that doing certain things would give them the results they want, I think most people would do it.

Call it a leap of faith. People get caught up in the, "Well what if I do it for a year and it doesn't work out?"

As Henry Ford says, "Whether you think you can or you think you can't, you're right."

I don't waste any time thinking about whether or not something could work. I just take every action possible to make it work and then if it doesn't, it's just an obstacle toward my goal. I stop, make a change in direction, and then keep on going.

Real Estate as Passive Income

I feel like real estate is among one of the easiest ways to generate passive income; easy in the sense that you don't need all the knowledge in your head. You can hire an agent to find the properties you want, those income-generating properties. From there you work with a settlement company and get the paperwork closed through a mortgage company. You can buy the house as long as you have the money. Hire a property manager who will manage your tenants and send you checks. When there are problems with your property manager will hire the contractor to take care of the problem.

When you have a network of people then all you need is the money to invest. When you park your money into a hard asset, one that you can see, touch, and walk into...then it starts giving you back money. That is better than anything else.

Luckily, Jim had the whole network already established for me. All I had to do was make the money and put it down. Even if I didn't have Jim's network, it wouldn't take more than a few hours to find the people that you need. People are really great about providing the services that are valuable to the marketplace. There are a few exceptions, obviously, but most of the time, you will find what you need.

You'll find the realtors you need who will help you locate the properties you want. Jim's program teaches you how to find those people. You then find the property manager and the contractors. Jim is great with teaching you those things. Once you learn how to form your network, you can do this business anywhere.

Jim taught me how to form it, but I was fortunate to be in his back yard, where he already had one formed. It's rather remarkable the service that he provides.

People can put that up as an obstacle, "I don't have a network," but that can be overcome. It's just an excuse. Think about it, your first day on the job, you don't really know anything about it, right? But, you learn, you ask questions, and a year into it, you're pretty proficient. It's no different with real estate investing.

Your job is to increase your financial intelligence to be able to set up your business and your network no matter where you are in this country. I think you can basically increase your own financial intelligence enough to be able to set this up wherever you are.

Barring some kind of physical abnormality that would keep you from even reading this book, I'm pretty sure that anybody can do this business.

Problems only grow to the amount of time you give them. I learned that when someone says, "I'll have this project in three months." Guess what? He'll have the project done in three months.

But if they said they could have it done in a week...they will have it done in a week. I learned this the hard way from college where I would wait until the last day to finish a project. I would get it done in one night. The problem will essentially grow to the amount of time you give it.

But, if you say, "I just need to get this done," and then you take action...action will get you there.

Get Rich Quick Scheme?

I know a lot of people think that real estate investing is some kind of "get rich quick" scheme. It's not. I don't think that there is anything such as a get rich quick opportunity except to get lucky, and that doesn't count!

I have always told my friends and coworkers, those who play the lottery, that if they win, it's cheating. That's how I feel about it. I would feel like I cheated and gave up on myself.

For me, life is about what you can make of it. Money isn't a great measurement of the value you bring to the marketplace. There is no "get rich quick", but there is "get poor quick" if you get roped into a scheme.

Real estate, however, is not a scheme. In my opinion, it is the absolute fastest way to accumulate money. It is a process for making money. There are absolute laws of making money. If you observe the laws of money, you will get wealthy. If not, you will be poverty-stricken. It goes back thousands of years.

So, no, real estate is *not* a get rich quick scheme. It's a very reliable way to get rich quickly. It's much better than a job or a career.

The sad truth is that many people don't want to be wealthy. They have become comfortable with where they are, and even if they can't admit it to themselves, they consciously know they would rather keep a comfortable lifestyle that they have. They're comfortable because it is familiar. That is safer than taking any kind of chance to change or become different. They may say they want to, but they don't really mean it.

So, what IS the right mindset?

Maybe I have an unfair advantage over people who have spent years in corporate America where they have been beaten down for years for trying something new and innovative. They've watched their 401k diminish in value and nothing is working for them. They're hoping to retire "soon" and yet that date just keeps moving out ahead of them.

They may still have years and years left before they can retire.

When they hear about real estate investing, maybe they've seen those smarmy late night TV commercials about the people sitting by their pools saying, "This, too, can be yours." The commercials are selling the dream, but not the process. Without the process, you're going to fail.

The truth is, real estate is a reliable way to make money if you follow a process, do things the right way and take the proper precautions.

By changing what goes into our minds, we can change where we are, and we can change what we are.

I don't claim to be above anyone at all. I think everyone is completely equal and has the same opportunity as I do. In order to get more, from wherever you are, you have to change what goes into your mind because when you change your input, you will change your output.

Motivation...a lot of people shy off of this, they say, "I'll get pumped up," but in two days I'll just be right back where I was.

I love this quote from Zig Ziglar, "Motivation isn't permanent, but neither is bathing." We still do it because it makes the quality of our life better and hope is so powerful. Hope and faith in the future. By creating a positive, compelling picture of the future for ourselves, we can get ourselves to do anything and that is truly exciting. The true excitement in life is our ability to make ourselves do the necessary things in order to achieve a certain result. I got really excited when I heard that. I didn't make that up, it came from Jim Rohn.

Everyone can be excited about that. We can make ourselves do the necessary things in order to get any result we want. It doesn't have to be what it has always been. We can change immediately. We just have to change what goes into our minds.

For example, in sales I've had times when things got really tough. There have been times when I've had to work one hundred hours a week for five or six weeks straight...there was a major problem in the company and this effort was required to sort it out. I was getting no sleep, and I was getting discouraged.

I realized that I had to find something to keep my mind focused on what I wanted it to be focused on. I learned from Jim Rohn that I shouldn't wish for things to be easier. I should wish for myself to be better. That's when I picked up the book, *The Greatest Salesman in the World.* That's basically a story about a person who had to read ten scrolls, each one for thirty days, three times a day. I decided to do that. By repeating these things in my mind, it conditioned my way of thinking. It made things easier and it made things better.

Obviously that took willpower and determination, but that is a great example of how to provide better input for my mind. I could have focused on the many hours I was working every week, but instead I focused on making myself better. I wanted to step up to the job.

We need this nourishment for our minds and we need that hope for the future because that fills us with a personal magnetism and passion that makes life worth living. That's such an incredible feeling.

Who Are You Spending Time With?

Look around you. Who are you spending your time with? I have a close group of friends, we're all saving together to buy another house. Three of these friends actually live in one of my houses that I own. They work with me in sales and they all want to buy their own houses.

I try to spend time around millionaires, because that's where I want to be. Soon, I'll start looking at spending time with billionaires, because I know already that's where I want to be.

We become more like the people we spend time with. The hardest thing I ever did was to separate myself, distance myself from my friends in high school. As hard as it was, I'm better for it.

Like attracts like.

If you fill your mind with thoughts of success, you will want to be around people who fill their thoughts with success. Most of the time when people fill their thoughts with success and goodwill, they are the wealthy people.

I'm twenty-four now and I got my first house when I was twenty-two. I went in half with my boss because I didn't have enough money to do it on my own. This is one of the "money-finding" tips...find someone to go in with you on an investment.

We bought a single family home with a bunch of rooms. It cost me $20,000 out of pocket for an expensive New Jersey house. I was splitting the mortgage with this guy, initially it was $1,170 a month. I brought in three roommates who were bringing in $1,500, so I was living with three other people and I was bringing home a couple hundred dollars.

Within a few months, I made some more money, so I bought my boss/partner out. I put down the other half of the house, which was $40,000.

It was a lot more than I needed or wanted to spend, but I owned the house now. My mortgage, taxes, and insurance were just under $1,200. I brought in a couple more people to live with me and the rent money shot up to $1,800 a month.

On a primary residence, where I was personally living, I had a $600 per month positive cash flow. For a first step, that was a really great. And yet, I did that wrong. I spent too much money.

I needed some education, and that is when I decided to take Jim's course. I learned everything Jim Toner had to teach. I worked with one of his Realtors and the next property I chose was a triplex. It required a down payment of $18,000. Out of pocket, after closing costs, it was $22,000. Monthly mortgage, taxes, insurance all came to $407. The rental income on it was already $1,410.

Right away I had a positive cash flow of $1,000!

I did have a couple of problems. Right away I had to evict a tenant. Then I had a water heater blow up that caused a $1,500 sewer bill and a few other minor things. Everything has evened itself out and I'm now back to a monthly cash flow of $900. That's a good thing.

Then I bought a duplex.

I actually bought it never having seen the inside. To this day, I haven't seen the inside of it and it is producing the best out of all three of my properties. When I got this, I contacted an investor who I knew had properties for investment income. I looked over the numbers he had for this property. I talked to the property manager and found that the tenants were good and reliable, having paid their rent for the past eight months. Taxes, insurance, and mortgage were $286. Two tenants and rental income was $1,100. One of my tenants was Section 8, and this was exciting. Even though my monthly payment was $290, my Section 8 check was $380, so I was guaranteed ninety dollars as long as I kept it up and clean. On top of that, I had the other rental income going up to $1,100. So, that has been producing income very nicely for the last seven months.

With those three houses I've been able to strictly budget my money so that I know what my living expenses are and they are covered 100% by my passive income. If I don't want to, I don't have to work anymore just to cover my monthly living expenses.

I still net $1,500 a month of additional spending money based on my $300,000 in assets that I've accumulated in just a couple of years.

Some people might call what I've managed to do "luck." But it isn't luck when you look at the numbers. When the numbers work, you know that it is a good business decision. I looked at the investor's list, made a decision within thirty minutes; we haggled for about forty-five minutes over the course of a couple of days. We worked the mortgage out. I spent maybe a total of ten hours of work and it brought in $4,000. I don't do anything now, the property manager calls me once a month to tell me that the tenants have paid, and that's it.

Haggling About Price

Unless you learn to haggle, you're not going to make a good real estate investor. My boss in sales taught me this. If you don't feel really uncomfortable asking for a price, then you're not asking for a good enough deal.

You should be asking what is in your best interest. It's not selfish. You need to be looking out for you. The other party is going to do the same.

Both sides need each other and you will come to a middle ground that works for both of you. There is no reason to give up any money.

The guy I was buying the property from has been a family friend for five years and he has taught me a lot about real estate. He's a real estate investor. That didn't stop me from saying, "I think I should offer you this much money because of A, B, and C."

In the end, I got a great deal. A lot better than I initially expected because I was willing to be uncomfortable with what I was offering. There is just no reason for you to give away your money.

If you hear a "no" then you can change your numbers if they still work for you. If, in the end, the deal is not good enough, you have to be willing to get up and walk away from the deal. There will be another one down the road.

I've closed about half of the deals I've put in offers on. That probably tells me that I don't lowball enough yet. I've put in eight offers, but I have gone through real estate investors who have the income producing properties. They've done most of the vetting and research for me.

Buying a House for Investment vs. Ownership

Real estate investing means you're looking for properties you're going to use as income producing properties. You're not looking to live there. Even if the property is below your standards, it is going to fit someone's needs.

I'm not saying you should become a "slum-lord". But you can buy houses that you don't particularly want to live in. That's fine. I'm providing a place for people to live and they are happy with their homes.

Remember that this is an investment vehicle. Look at the numbers. Eliminate any money-eating problem properties. Buy something that is neat, clean, and up to code. I don't care what color the living room is, I care how much rent will be coming in. That demonstrates a mindset change from being a home buyer to being a real estate investor. Buying a home is like getting yourself a good pet. You'll play with the puppy because you want to make sure it loves you. Buying an asset, it's like a check out at a store. There is a lot of emotion in buying a house you'll be living in. there should be no emotion involved in buying an investment. If the numbers work, then take action.

Be Who You Want To Be

Just remember, you can turn your life into anything you desire. Know that. Believe that. You can turn your life into anything you desire, so don't settle for less than all you can be. The way you do that is to find people in your life who are living the way you want to live. Befriend them. Ask them how they got to where they are.

Form a relationship with and then study the kind of people they are. Anyone can turn themselves into any type of person they want to be. Why settle for less? Do the things you need to do to become more like them.

You don't have to be the same person you are today. You can be whoever you want tomorrow. Change what goes into your mind and you will change who you are.

It's a scientific fact. It's not luck. It's not chance.

Case Study – Josh Meeder

I had an early start in my financial education. I've been licensed to sell insurance and financial products since I was eighteen. My father had an insurance agency that I took over after I graduated from college. He passed away from mesothelioma when I was a senior in college. He got lung cancer from cutting brake pads for only two months in a summer job when he was fourteen.

I jumped into being self-employed from the time I graduated college. At the time I left the one company I was working for, I was top in the nation in sales in the top five percent. I went to a different company, started it up, and grew it to about one-hundred fifty employees in three states. It was a big operation.

From there, I went to Chicago and managed large-scale enterprise software, until I was downsized. At that point, I came back to Pennsylvania where I started a marketing and advertising company. I went from being on the bottom rung to director of client services managing about $65 million worth of sales and marketing for a lot of internationally known companies. I was downsized from that right before Christmas in 2008.

That was a really bad time. I had a large farm with a big mortgage and no income.

I've had the entrepreneurial bug most of my life, and when I heard about Jim Toner's seminar on the radio I knew that this was something I wanted to do.

Actually, I'd heard of Jim, he had been on the radio for several years. I went to one of his seminars and I really liked what he had to say. Not only was he a local guy in that he absolutely knew what he was talking about in real estate in this area, he was also a good guy.

He wasn't just interested in making money in real estate. He was about bettering yourself and making a difference in people's lives. That's what attracted me. Jim rehabbed and gave away two homes to returning war veterans and I saw some of the national coverage on that.

I really liked the approach he had with that. When I met Jim, we just hit it off very well. Everything he said just made sense to me.

My Start in Real Estate Investing

My very first project was a home flip.

I went through Jim's course and right away I started my first flip. It was a total of three and a half months from purchase to sale, including the rehab. I made $14,000 on my first sale.

It absolutely saved my financial life!

I risked what I had left to get this one going and it made all the difference. This was back in 2009 and I have been doing residential flips and right now I recently started a large commercial project that is a mixture of businesses, a health and wellness center, and I'm rehabbing a 130 year-old opera house to put this in with an attached greenhouse and a whole bunch of different businesses.

I've done five residential flip properties and one large commercial development.

What Housing Slump?

My first flip was in 2009, and we were well into the "housing slump" so that should tell people that real estate investing is the real deal if you know what you're doing.

One of the first things I learned in the course is that the largest and most stable markets in real estate are your first-time home buyers and entry-level home ownership. A lot of people are always looking to get out of renting. If you can provide quality, affordable housing you'll do well.

Through Jim's program I learned about discipline and the formula to follow, because otherwise I would not have had a clue about how to do it otherwise. I went in, I found that the numbers worked according to the formula Jim showed me. I went through all the various steps of looking at properties in a certain zip code that have been selling very quickly.

Once I found a good zip code area that I liked, I found the right house, evaluated the numbers, and I put in the offer. I got the house for a very fair price. It took under $10,000 to buy the three-bedroom brick house in the city. It was in a neighborhood that wasn't the best, but it was making a comeback and had some really nice attributes.

I fixed up the house, and I'll admit that I made mistakes along the way, but still stuck to the numbers and the formula and was able to make between $14,000 to $15,00 in three months.

I had the feeling that this was the right thing to do for me. I knew the course and program that Jim had put forth were financially sound and for me it worked financially. I followed his directions and it gave me everything I was hoping for.

That made a ***huge*** difference in my life.

Setting Up My Circle of Experts

Because I had already been in business before, I had a lot of my own experts established. I had my accountants and I had a really great real estate agent who was the right type of agent. Jim described absolutely everything in the program, what I needed and how to find them.

I can't stress enough how important it is to use the right kind of real estate agent. When you're into real estate investment, you want to work with an agent who works primarily or exclusively with investors, or one who has done rehabs or owns property on their own. They just know how to look at it differently.

A "retail" real estate agent sells pretty houses to people who are looking to buy "pretty houses." That type of agent would walk into the houses we are considering as an investment and say, "Oh my gosh! The ceiling is falling down! There is no plumbing! No one should ever buy this!"

Those are the types of agents you need to stay away from. You want to find a real estate agent who knows the numbers, knows the community, and can show quantitatively that houses in this market are selling at a certain price in a certain time frame and they can do the leg work.

There is a fair amount of work that you require of an agent over a normal buyer, but when you establish the right relationship, it comes back four-fold to them because they get not only the commission from the purchase, but they get the commission from the full retail sale. With that in mind, I've done probably five properties in that time and that is just my business and my personal purchases.

Because I've focused on flips, I've been a very great client for my real estate agent!

You have to look for someone who understands the investor mindset and has either done it themselves or works with people who are doing it. If not, it is just too hard to educate them about your needs.

Entrepreneurial Mindset

I came from an entrepreneurial background being self-employed most of my life. I can see the value in taking a risk. I'm also well-versed, or handy with building, so I know some of the contracting trades. It is very easy for me to see the potential of a place.

As long as it is in the right neighborhood and the comparative sales and the time on the market are right, within a specific radius depending on your location. If the numbers are there, then your market will support it. I like this very quantitative, data-driven approach to real estate investing.

This is one of the things that I really love about Jim's approach. You take all the emotion out of it. Either the house works or it doesn't. The neighborhood works or it doesn't. Right up front he said, "You may have to put in ten offers before you even get one accepted. But when you get an offer accepted, the money is already made.

That's the key to this entire business. Know your numbers and make sure you make your money when you buy, not when you sell!

As I said, I've made mistakes. I think all real estate investors do. At one point I had gotten too many properties at once, mainly because I got so excited about it. I needed to have someone take one of the properties off my hands, so I took someone who had never done anything like this in her life.

I said, "Hey, I'm going to show you what Jim taught me. I'll help you through it." She has had no experience in real estate, or setting up her own business. I showed her the ropes, got her in touch with the contractors that I was using and she was able to re-do the entire house. She did an entire flip herself and she made a couple bucks doing it. She did well with it.

Getting Started – Avoiding Pitfalls

First off, get a mentor.

I'm serious. Get a mentor.

It's certainly possible to be successful as a real estate investor, but more people fail than succeed when they don't know what to watch out for. I've talked to a lot of people who know I'm a real estate investor and they come to me with deals, thoughts, suggestions, and plans.

What I see is people making all the same kinds of mistakes over and over, the same mistakes that I would have made if I didn't have a mentor.

I firmly believe in mentoring.

The best NBA players aren't self-directed. They have great coaches, specialized coaches for throwing, passing, or shooting, or whatever the sport is.

Mentoring is the best way to avoid a lot of pitfalls, which usually translate to losing money. Just one or two pitfalls in a single project can cost you your entire profit of the project.

One of the biggest pitfalls I see unmentored or inexperienced real estate investors make is not quantifying the market properly. They haven't done the right research, haven't checked out the sold comprehensive sales in the immediate area for like, kind, and quality properties, to see how fast homes are moving in that area. From this information, the investor can know what they can realistically expect to make on the sale of the property.

What often happens to a lot of inexperienced people is that they get romantically attached to a property or to a neighborhood and they feel that their property is more valuable than it realistically is. It will take longer to sell at that price.

As an investor, you want your properties to sell quickly, so they need to be priced at the mid- to low- point so that there is no problem.

Let me give you an example:

The first house that I did was when I fixed it up all told it was an $85,000 house. It was a 4-bedroom, 2-1/2 bath house. These homes were selling very quickly. When I pulled my house up on the MLS it was the only one that had a brand-new kitchen, all new tile, new laminate flooring, new carpet, new bathroom, lighting fixtures...everything in my rehabbed home was brand new.

So, when someone would ask their real estate agent to find houses in this area for under $100,000, there was nothing comparable with what I had to offer. It was a great property. It was well priced and I got a contract in six days because I priced it properly to move quickly.

This all sounds fine, but I want you to picture what this house looked at when I bought it. The word "crack house" comes to mind. It was pretty bad. The doors were barred shut for closure, the ceiling was falling down, all the copper plumbing had been ripped out leaving gaping holes in the wall, rusted furnace. You name it, and it was wrong. The average person walking into that home would have been frightened.

I looked at it and saw that it was structurally sound. Based on the training I got from Jim on how to look at a property both from a repair standpoint and a structural standpoint, I knew the house had good bones. I did have a property inspection done so that I would be aware of any major issues going on, and allowed for these in my rehab budget.

Because I knew what I was doing, I knew the numbers, knew what to expect in the rehab, and knew what the selling price was likely to be, I would say it was greatly successful.

To complete the example, I paid just $9,990 to purchase the house. You have to understand that we are in a unique situation in Pittsburgh, where the market never really dropped out. We have been very, very stable and housing is affordable here, so there are a lot of great deals.

I allowed for between $35,000 and $40,000 for rehab.

Further, I knew that I could expect to sell the house for around $85,000.

My profit on this home was in the range of $35,000.

I'm NOT Crazy!

When I first got into real estate investing, people thought I was absolutely out of my mind. Remember, I was out of work; I'd just been terminated from a very high-paying executive job. I had a 30-acre farmhouse that was falling down around my ears that was very expensive to maintain. I basically had to leverage what I had left to make everything work.

I risked everything and it did work for me. I didn't have a contingency plan. It **had** to work.

I went to work on this with full faith that it would work. There was no option that it couldn't work.

For me, it was a matter of attitude and belief in the process and in myself. One of the things that Jim suggests, and I believe it whole-heartedly, is that the only things that change you over time are the people you meet and the books you read.

For me, the more I read Napoleon Hill's *Think and Grow Rich*, the more I learned that it was about attitude and perseverance and having the right mental approach to it.

I'll be the first to tell you that real estate investing is not an easy gig. The TV shows make it look easy and glamorous. This is a business. It's not a "get rich quick" idea. It is time consuming and at times can be very frustrating, just as any business can be.

You have to do your homework, do your research, and know your numbers. And, in the beginning, you will be the one doing it all. You just can't outsource some of this work.

You need to go inspect the properties, the neighborhoods, put in the offers, meet with the contractors, and understand the contracts you're writing.

What you don't want to do is be on site every single day as the rehab work is being done. Even if you're skilled at it, swinging a hammer next to your contractor is a big waste of your time. But, you should have a basic understanding of the rehabbing process, or at least pick it up through the process what it means to need certain plumbing and electrical work done.

You are ultimately responsible for knowing the building codes or permitting requirements. Your contractor should know this, but you are ultimately responsible. Knowing these kinds of things will make you a more effective investor.

As a real estate investor, you will run into a lot of setbacks, from cost overruns, problems with contractors and other unforeseen things. As soon as you open up a wall, you usually get a surprise you weren't expecting.

What It Takes to Be Successful

There are three things you absolutely must do in order to be successful as a real estate investor:

- First and foremost, attitude is what will determine your success or failure, attitude and mindset.
- Secondly, get yourself a coach or the right education and support systems.
- The third part is really getting your business in line. This means you have to have the right structure for your accounting or your entity, having your banking in line, where you can get the funding that you will require.

Real estate investing is a constant learning experience. There is always something new to learn in all businesses, and real estate investing is no different. I've done five flips and I feel like I'm only about a quarter of the way to where I should be in order to do this on a continual basis.

I've heard some folks say that it could take thirty or forty properties to get this dialed in and nailed down to where it becomes transactional. I'm learning on every project, but the learning curve is shortened by having the right education and mentorship.

The other thing to be careful about is beginning to think that you are indispensable to the entire process. You'll just bog the process down because you're not looking at the big picture.

You've hired an expert in the contractor that you're partnering with. You have to believe in your experts.

Your contract needs to be structured so that you have the right milestones and expectations in place so you can manage the contractor and contract rather than the actual physical work.

You don't want to be on site every day and you definitely don't want to be doing all the physical work. If you insist on doing this, it will delay your project and anything that stretches out the project is a waste of money.

You lose money when you are the one doing the physical work.

The Process

In order to find the right property, you will probably pull between one and two hundred listings in a specific zip code, or have your agent do it.

From those listings, I will choose the top twenty that I think I might be interested in. there are certain things you're looking for, and you'll find these out in the course or from your mentor.

I'll do a drive-by on all of these properties, and I'll pick between five and seven that I want to go inside and inspect. Of these, I will put in an offer on one.

Once you find the right property, you will have put in between five and eight hours of work looking at listings, doing drive-bys, and checking out between eight and twelve properties.

Once the deal is signed, you have some time to meet with your contractors, your general contractor...you may have HVAC, plumbing, electrical, and some work in submitting the permits if you're the one doing that.

You might have to spend a couple of hours with your contractor going over everything you want handled so that they give you an adequate bid. If you don't have an established contractor relationship, you may end up going through two or three contractors (which will take up between six and eight hours) in order to get an adequate bid on the property rehab.

Once everything is in line, I would personally be on site two times a week for an hour or two checking with the contractor, making sure they have what they need and that they have, making sure they have what they need and that things are all progressing along at a pace that makes sense for the overall timeline.

Progress is almost always determined by how well you construct your contracts. You put milestones into the contract, and the more milestones you have, tying them off to the release of funds or compensation, the better off you are.

I can pretty much say, that for those contractors who want 100% of their money up front, I tell them, "Have a nice day." And, I just find another one. You're the one signing the check, you have the power. There are a lot of very good contractors out there who are looking for work. There are also quite a few unscrupulous contractors out there, so be sure to do your homework. Call references, check their work from other projects, and structure your contract so that it protects you.

I learned that in Jim's course. You want a really good, tight contract because when a dispute arises, that is the only governing document you have to fall back on.

Jim's course provides a lot of sample documentation that he has developed and used over the years so you're not starting from scratch. That was a tremendous asset to me just starting out in this business, having those documents and contracts that he offers.

By taking Jim's course I saved myself a lot of money and a lot of time. He did all the research I needed tracking down the proper things I needed in order to make a good deal.

That's one of the biggest reasons I'm key on mentorship. Looking back, I would have easily made mistakes by not going through the course that would have cost me a lot more than the tuition I paid.

As an entrepreneur, I understand how important it is to follow in the footsteps of someone who has gone before me. There are plenty of really smart people who have been really successful in their careers who look at real estate investing like it's some kind of simple business. They think that it's not all that hard, until they make mistakes.

Just one or two mistakes can cost you your entire profit on a property. I can't stress that enough. Those TV shows that show all these home flippers who make it look so easy, they're doing the general public a real disservice because they make light of some of the problems that just "get fixed" without showing the viewer everything that goes into the fix.

Sure, it's possible that it can go that smoothly, for someone who has done between fifty and a hundred flips. For the average new real estate investor, it's not going to go that smoothly.

It just isn't.

We've all seen those programs where they have one or two people doing the work and within a half an hour they show you the highlights of buying a house and making $35,000 with very little work.

They're making it seem too good to be true, and it is because that isn't the real picture of what flipping and rehabbing a house is like.

Now, real estate has that potential, but some of those programs really glamorize it and make anyone think that they can do it and none of those programs emphasize how important it is to have someone who knows what they're doing, like having a coach or a mentor.

They make it look like anyone can walk out, buy a house, fix it up, and sell it for a huge profit. I think it is a huge mistake to do that without the right support or training.

Your attitude and belief that you will succeed will see you through as long as you don't have too big an ego that will prevent you from taking advice or seeking an education from someone who has already done what you're seeking to do.

When you know what to expect and can prepare for it, you're going to have a better chance at success, too.

If I had the chance to change anything at all about my real estate investing journey, it would be to follow the program a little bit closer than I did.

I hate to put myself in a bad light, but while I made good money on my first project, I could have actually made another $5,000 if I had followed Jim's process a little more closely.

I needed a new furnace and my general contractor (who worked out real well for me) recommended someone he had worked with in the past, but not recently. He knew he did good work.

My mistake was in taking this guy's word for it and hiring the guy without checking him out. He came in, gave me a price and said, "Hey, I can get started this weekend as I have an opening in my schedule. My only problem is I don't have the funds in the bank to get the furnace for you. If you can give me 80% up front, I'll get it started this weekend and then I will bill you for the rest."

That's absolutely a violation of what Jim taught me.

I did as the guy wanted, and he took the money and ran.

I got ripped off all that money and haven't been able to recover it. If I had listened more carefully and followed Jim's advice more closely, I could have avoided that loss.

What I should have done was turn the guy down, or go to the furnace store myself and put the money on the furnace. I didn't. I trusted too much, made a rash decision and it cost me money.

You live and learn, and some of us have to learn the hard way.

Buying and Flipping vs. Buying and Holding

Up to now, I've really gone for the flips, but I'm changing my mindset a bit now. The thing I liked about Jim's course is that it gave me a couple of options based on where I was in my life.

There is wholesaling, which is the easiest entry into the market where you don't have to have as much capital requirement, and anyone can do it.

Then there is flipping, requiring a much bigger financial commitment, but has a greater cash reward immediately.

Then there is the buy and hold strategy where I will rehab a property and then rent it for long-term income.

When I first started in this business, I was in a very poor financial state, so I needed to get those cash infusions and that is why I went directly to the rehab/flip market. As I've improved my financial situation, I am now looking at the "buy and hold" market, the rental strategy.

This is what has led me to the commercial project that I'm working on now. This is outside the scope of what Jim teaches, but his course gave me the basis to start it. I bought a 13,000 square foot historic building in the hometown that I grew up in, an old opera house from the 1880s.

I've been renovating it. The plan is to make it a bit of a "give back" to the community. There is a community based health and wellness and events center. We start it up, start and support local businesses that are socially and economically concerned or responsible. It is called the "Center of Harmony."

We are able to offer several people from the community an opportunity to give back and start their businesses, so we have a coffee shop, a domestic and organic sourced yarn and knitting supply shop, handmade jeweler and metal smith, equestrian apparel, a doctor of integrative medicine and medical acupuncture, a locally made wine store, and a greenhouse that I'm trying to fill. I also offer free electronic recycling for the community.

It's like a unique mini-mall where we can do some really unique things and hold special events there. We have a 3000 square foot opera hall and meeting hall, so we can hold seminars, we have had a monk from India coming to do Tibetan medicine, wedding receptions, and all sorts of things. It is really a great project. My girlfriend, Dana, is largely responsible for the project. She is drawn to a health-conscious, eco-conscious lifestyle.

So this is where I am now, able to give back to the community with that. The buy and hold rental strategy is the beginning of my rental portfolio so I have current and residual income moving forward in trying to stay out of ever having to get a J-O-B again.

Giving Back

What really attracted me to Jim in the beginning was his charity work and his give back attitude designed to improve the lives of those around him. That struck a chord with me and that is what we're doing now with the opera house refurb.

I'm just glad to be in a position to be able to do this. It's really, really important to give back to the community as an entrepreneur. It might be doing what I'm doing; it might be that you become a Big Brother or a Big Sister to someone who needs to be mentored, as long as there is something outside yourself that you find fulfillment with.

Through Jim, I met Frank McKinney. This guy is an amazing real estate investor. He's also an author with three best-selling books in three different categories. This guy went from being kicked out of four different high schools to being a guy who has made millions of dollars. But his question for himself is, "Where am I going in life?"

He found charity work to be soothing for his soul. He started the Caring House Foundation, which Jim is a board member of, and they build a sustainable village in Haiti just about every year. This means housing for fifty people, a church and community center, and I think a school or a hospital.

Frank has done this, and has built over 7500 homes for the poorest of the poor in Haiti and that is what motivates him.

When I went to Jim's presentation, I learned about Frank McKinney and his Caring House Foundation. I remember thinking, "Someday I'm going to know that guy." He was someone I wanted to be like.

Through Jim I met Frank and donated a house in Haiti.

This journey has been amazing. From just a little over three years ago I went from being terminated from my job and being at the end of my financial rope to making a change and meeting someone as influential as Frank.

I've always been positive, and have learned to surround myself with positive people. I had faith that Jim's program would do for me what I needed it to do.

When I think about what might have been preventing this kind of success in my life before, I can only pinpoint my fear and doubt in myself. When I let go of a dream, I allowed fear and doubt to creep in. Those two things kill your dreams, because they are now your reality.

What you think about, you bring about.

What I'd like for you to take away from reading this chapter is that if you don't take the risk, you'll never know just how successful you could be in this business.

It is a calculated and manageable or measureable risk. There is a history of success behind this risk. It is not get rich quick; it is not a fly-by-night operation.

Real estate investing is a time-tested financially proven system to improve our financial situation.

It's also one of the biggest opportunities you'll ever have to make change in the world. I'm able to make a difference in the lives of the people I sell to and rent to. I am able to provide affordable quality housing to people who need it.

Every time you take a distressed property and rehab it, you've done a great service for that neighborhood. You have turned an eyesore into a home where a new family will take up residence. It changes a lot of lives.

There is a tremendously powerful impact when you look at the whole scope of what you're actually doing. The biggest impact you can have is with the neighbors around you.

Get the attitude right. Line up your coach or mentor. Get your business in order and find your way to funding your projects. Our country has a severe lack of financial literacy. Learning about finances and loans might be the biggest challenge for new investors to overcome.

Now get out there, negotiate the deals, and be comfortable doing it!

Case Study – Ken George

My first real estate investment activity was when I bought my first house, my own personal residence for $24,000 and lived in it for four years. When I sold it as a rent-to-own, I got $54,000 for it. And this was before I took any of Jim Toner's classes.

My next house, the one I did immediately after Jim's classes I used a private money lender and made a really good profit on that. I don't live in Pittsburgh, so the market here is a little different, and I've had a bit of a learning curve.

We were taught to use a circle of experts, and so I hired someone who would take care of contacting contractors and getting things done on the properties that I purchased, but that didn't work out the way I'd expected.

Initially, I made some really good money to begin with, but I think I may have expanded my real estate investing business too quickly, and we haven't been hitting them really well lately, so we're reevaluating our approach.

At first we were buying rentals, and it wasn't giving us the kind of return we were looking for. We were learning to deal with tenants, and we had some who had fallen on hard times, one in the hospital. It's hard to collect the rent from those kinds of tenant.

We had also been using a private money lender and selling homes on a rent-to-own basis, but that wasn't working quite as well as we would have liked. I know that this is the best idea in terms of long-term income coming in.

We're both working full-time jobs and have two kids. We do as much as we can at a home base, but for us we are still looking for a system that really works for us. We have certainly made some money doing this.

Last year we did four good flips. One I bought for $10,000 and then sold it for $17,500 in a single day. I made $7,500 in one day! That, so far, has been my best real estate investing day.

I bought another one for $7,000 and then sold it for $12,500 and that wasn't too bad. We made some profit after all was said and done, but not as much as we would have liked. Still, we made over $3,000 in about three weeks. I don't make $1,000 a week at my job, so it can still pay better than my job.

Business Line of Credit

When we first started, we had a $20,000 business line of credit that we used as our seed money. With that, we were able to go out and buy a couple of those deals. It was great to be able to write that check for $10,000 and then realize the profit right away. We repaid the line of credit and then put the extra in our account.

The next couple of projects we did the same thing, we took money out of our line of credit, and then when we flipped the house we repaid it and deposited the profit.

Growing Too Fast

After a few really good flips, I think we got too excited and wanted to grow our business too fast. We went out and bought marketing materials, then got a couple of credit cards to do work on the properties because we were keeping them. But I think that hurt us, trying to keep trying to keep the properties instead of cashing them in after getting them refurbished.

Another thing we've been doing is buying lease options where we take over other people's payments. Whenever you take over someone else's payments, then you try to rent it back out, but again, we were running into problems because people are pretty stretched and if our tenants can't pay the rent, we're covering the mortgage payments.

You have to keep these rentals for a long time in order to get them paid down enough to make them worth something.

We really prefer to buy something for a low price with our line of credit, fix it up, and then in a month or two sell it and pay yourself back. This is an interesting lesson, a hard lesson to learn, but it's all part of the business.

It's hard to say no to a rental when it's literally in your back yard. I don't want to sell them when they make perfect rentals and I don't have to hire a property manager to handle them. I can take care of the property and manage it without having to hire anyone.

But then we are the ones who have to see if our tenant who is in the hospital has a boyfriend or family member who can send us a check. That's one of the interesting parts of this business, and being a landlord isn't everyone.

The other thing about rentals is you have to make sure you know your area and the demand for the types of rentals you buy. Because we're further away from the Pittsburgh area, we are not able to command the same kind of rental rates they do in the city unless it's corporate. This is something that we're trying to get more of by advertising to them, calling them up and letting them know we have rental properties.

My focus now is figuring out how to get higher priced renters and getting ideal tenants.

We've tried wholesaling, but we don't have as much of a market as you might in a bigger metropolitan area.

You have to try different strategies so that we're providing what people need a make enough money to make this business worthwhile. We have discovered that you have to really check people's references because people will say all kinds of things to get you to hire them, but then they don't work out.

While this is a business easy enough that anyone can do it, something you have to keep in mind is that it is a business.

As with any business, you have to be really motivated to make it work. You also have to know where your money is at all times, whether a choice is the best use of your money or not.

We once hired someone to help us turn over properties. One day, we came in to check on a property and discovered that her husband was there doing the electrical work. He wasn't an electrician and he was doing it all wrong. I suggested he do it a different way and he got angry and just left the job.

Surrounding yourself with a circle of knowledgeable experts is a big part of your job and it isn't always easy. We've found, in our area, that it is hard to find good people who know their stuff and are willing to do it for a fair price.

We've had our fair share of people who get angry with us for one reason or another and damage our properties. That's just really frustrating. Our best tenants are usually the corporate people or government people who pay their rent on time and take care of the property.

It's golden when you have tenants who take good care of your property. That's what all real estate investors want. So our focus now is finding high quality people to work with and to rent to.

I'm still working to build the kind of business Jim taught where I work *on* the business rather than *in* the business. Right now, because we're not finding good quality contractors, we have had to do a lot of the work ourselves. That's not the right way to do it.

The Future

I know it sounds a little like I'm sour on real estate investing, but I'm not. I recognize that I've made a couple of mistakes based on my earlier successes. We tried to expand too quickly, didn't evaluate our market as well as we should have, and have learned we need to screen our tenants better than we have.

The thing is, I'm only 28. I was told at work that I'm maxed out. My wife and I both work full-time and have enough to afford a house and some nice cars. But we're not living a really extravagant lifestyle. I didn't want to be sixty-something and being in the same place. So the only way I'm going to make a difference in my life is to make my real estate investing business a success.

And it doesn't become a fully functioning business overnight. We're looking at the future, and that means our long-range goals include getting twelve properties in our portfolio. If we can generate about $1,000 a month from each property, that will mean $144,000 a year in income, without working.

That's a really nice income!

But it isn't going to happen overnight. We're just getting started. We know it works, and we've discovered where we have made a few mistakes. So, we have to keep our eyes on that future where residual income will provide a living income for us, whether we're in our 40s or in our 80s. That makes for a really great retirement income!

I know one guy who is a real estate investor. He saves all his money until he has all the cash he needs to buy a house. He renovates it, rents it and all that income is residual because he doesn't have to pay a mortgage. He continues to save, and in a couple years he buys another house the same way.

Pretty soon, this method started to snowball and he was buying houses a bit faster. By the time you have five houses paid off, you're generating something like $4,000 to $5,000 a month.

I made the mistake of trying to buy them first and get the cash flow later. So, I'm changing my approach because the way I was doing it was OK, until we had a hiccup...and one single hiccup can derail your whole train. You have to have those hiccups covered.

The thing with real estate investing, it does generate money. But it is not a super-fast way of doing it. It's a business and you have to treat it like a business.

Jim started out living in a dumpy apartment, sitting on plastic lawn chairs. He had nothing, and look at what he's managed to do. I've only been in the business for a short time. By the time I've been in the business as long as Jim, I expect I will be in a similar position.

I haven't stopped learning about real estate investing. You can do something one time and it works out perfectly. Then you do it again and things don't go quite so well.

Don't stop learning. Build friends going up because when you run into tough times, they will be there to support you and help you out. I have close friends and family who are fully behind me. I don't know what I would do without them.

On the tough days, I remember making $7,500 in a single day. There is no way I will ever do that at my current job. So, it's up to me to make it happen again. At least in real estate investing it's possible.

Case Study – Staci and Derrik Kuhns

We got into real estate investing because we were looking for something that we could get into to make extra money and be able to work on it together. We landed on the idea of investing in real estate.

I'm the kind of person who can do things hand-on and work with my hands, so we decided we wanted to buy houses, fix them up and sell them or rent them out.

What I found out, after talking to people who had been in the business is that a lot of people are actually in the investment real estate business and aren't doing very well at it. Yet, there are people out there who are doing very, **very** well at it.

So the question was why are some people more successful and others aren't?

The simple answer is that the people who were not making money at it were doing it wrong.

We heard about Jim's program and realized that there is more to this real estate investing business than the average person knows, things you **need** to know. The system Jim uses makes it easy and makes this business available to anyone. You don't have to be a handyman to do the job. I found it is more profitable to not do this work on my own because now I have more time for other things.

Initially we were interested in building a portfolio of rental properties. But one day, I saw a house that I thought would make for a perfect flip. I came home and told my wife about it and that I was going to put in an offer on it.

At her look of dismay I said, "Don't worry, I'm going to lowball the offer. We won't get it."

This is what my wife wanted to hear because we were working on other rentals and we knew we didn't have a whole lot of money to put into a flip. Despite my assurances that we wouldn't get the house, deep inside I hoped we would get it because it was a really great house and it wasn't going to take a lot of money to refurb it.

You guessed it. We got the house.

This was a big step for us. I think we had a little bit of fear about flipping a house, and as Jim says, "Fear is your biggest drawback." We had done all our homework, we had a mentor in Jim, we knew what to do, what not to do, how to buy the house, how to make the deal, and so we were here on the verge of our first flip property.

Most of what we learned from Jim, especially in the beginning, helped to take away the fear of the unknown about real estate investing. But, we still had to step out there and actually do it.

Derrik Trump

When I first told people that we were getting into real estate investing, they just joked about it. People at work would tease me, calling me Derrik "Trump" and then go on to say, "You're going to lose everything."

They couldn't believe we were going to do this in such a bad housing market.

We made $47,000 on that deal...that's what ended up in our pocket.

When I put in the offer, I offered them $50,000 for the property. It was a real low-ball offer, but I knew this was part of the game. Any time I had a question or concern, I knew I could call Jim and we would talk back and forth and work things out.

With this house, Jim's words were running through my head. I saw this house for sale, a foreclosure. This happened a lot when the market was dropping and many people were afraid of buying anything in this market.

Here's a secret for you...even in the worst housing market, people still need a good home at a decent price. It doesn't matter how good or bad the economy is...prices can go up and down. If you provide a good home for a good price, you will have buyers.

The biggest trick is to not be greedy.

I know, that seems like a funny statement to make when I just told you how much money we made on that first flip. But we made that much because we weren't greedy.

During the time I was evaluating that house I saw three other homes that were similar in style, construction, and all under foreclosure. There were also three homes that had regular For Sale signs in the front yard.

It was a really nice neighborhood in a small town, perfect for young families. These were ideal starter homes for young families. I looked at one of the foreclosed properties and noticed that there was a blue tarp up on a little part of the roof.

That's when I said to myself, "I smell money." To me, that blue tarp on the roof said that when someone lost their home the bank took it over, and a piece of the roof blew off and it was now leaking. I needed to know just how bad this leak was.

I called my Realtor and said, "Hey, let's go take a look at this house." As soon as I told my Realtor the address, she said, "I've been in that house, and there is one part of the bedroom upstairs where the roof got blown off a little bit and there is some water damage."

No surprise there. I said, "Well then, I **definitely** want to see this house." Over the years I've learned that real estate agents do not understand investors. A real estate agent is used to bringing in somebody who simply wants to buy a house. They don't understand that investors look at properties differently.

I'm looking for a way to make some money. Real estate agents look at houses as a place someone is going to move into tomorrow. Anything that keeps them from moving in is a strike against that house.

I spent about half an hour in that house and apart from the water damage the house was beautiful. I went upstairs and saw that the bedroom ceiling was coming down in wet pieces. I knew immediately that they were not going to sell that house.

At the time they had it on the market, they were asking $80,000 for it.

There is no way in the world that a young family is going to see all that damage in the bedroom and want to move into that house. There were five other houses in the neighborhood for sale that did not have that kind of damage. A young family looking for a starter home is not interested in roofing problems and water damage.

Before I even looked at that house, I had asked my Realtor a few questions that also helped my decision. She gave me some comps for the area and saw that houses this size were selling in this area and for a very nice price.

Because of the roof and water damage I knew that no one would buy that house unless they were an investor. I looked at the rest of the house, going from the upstairs all the way to the basement. I knew how much money I would have in that house if I were to buy it for myself. My cost estimate for repairs came to between $5,000 and $7.000 including fixing the roof, the ceiling in the bedroom, and a few other little things.

The average home buyer is not interested in putting that much money into a house they plan to live in. They want it "move-in ready" without problems.

Once I came up with the rehab numbers I compared those to the comps of similar homes in the area. Then, keeping in mind that I was working on a couple of rentals at the same time, I put in a real low-ball offer, firmly believing that I wouldn't get it. I almost guaranteed my wife that we wouldn't get that house.

The guys at work were really hassling me, telling me that I was going to lose my shirt. Then we got the call from the Realtor, our offer had been accepted. Once we completed the rehab, we compared it to the other similar houses in the area. According to those, we could probably get $160,000 on that house.

But, at that price, I knew the house would sit on the market for a long time. I'm not in the business to sit and hold houses that I have to pay any kind of mortgage on. We decided to **not** be greedy and decided to make a $20,000 to $30,000 profit on the house.

We had a buyer for that house within a couple months of buying it. During that time, we were renovating the house. When it was done, it was absolutely beautiful. I would have enjoyed living in that house.

We made $47,000 on the sale of that house. That's a lot of money to make in two months.

During that same time, the other houses on the street, same size, same builder, priced quite a bit higher, are still available. The asking price for those houses was somewhere around $140,000 to $150,000. I knew that if I priced my house cheaper, it would sell a lot quicker.

When you look at a deal, you should already know how much you need to sell it for. When you take into account your rehab costs, you know what you should offer for the house.

If your offer is rejected, don't feel badly. There's another deal just around the corner.

The woman who bought the house had two or three kids and as a single mom, she was absolutely delighted with her beautiful home.

Now, a bit of information for you...when we were ready to list the house, our Realtor tried to get us to raise our price. We wanted to list at $128,000. She knew what the other two homes were selling for and told us that we were listing at a price that was far too low.

My answer to her was, "And the whole time, they're still sitting there. Empty. Not sold. I bought this house as an investment. You know what I bought it for, but you don't know what I've put into it. If I'm happy making this kind of profit pricing it at $128,000, then we're listing it at $128,000.

You're going to get "experts" who think they know better than you do. Some of those experts will steer you wrong. We were delighted with our profit in that flip. That's how this business works.

We have sold other houses and made $10,000 to $15,000. That is a nice profit on a house project. But that $47,000 has been our best profit yet. It reminds us every day that it can be done.

Especially when everyone is telling you it can't be done.

They don't tease me too much at work about being Derrik "Trump" anymore.

Making a House a Home

We learned a lot on that flip, but I find that when we're looking for properties, whether they're for rental or to flip, we are still looking in the same types of areas. You want to become a little bit of an expert in an area; you want to know if homes are even selling where you find a really great deal on a house.

So, location is really important. You might find a really great deal, but if the location isn't doing well in terms of other sales, it doesn't matter how much you put into a house, you're going to have trouble getting your money out of it.

Now, I will say that we would do more for a home we plan to flip than one we might plan to rent. We might do extra landscaping or put a nice fence around the place, something that will catch a buyer's eye to make them want to take a look at the house. I probably wouldn't do that if it were going to be a rental.

Now, we **do** work to make our rentals very appealing because we know that is going to be someone's home. We renovate places to the point that we would be willing to move into it. The last thing in the world we want to be are slumlords. We would always make it to where if I could bring my children into this house, then we can rent this house.

From time to time we have had tenants we have had to get rid of, but most of our rentals are absolutely beautiful and that attracts really good tenants. We've had people move in who put their own money into the landscaping. They want to make their home beautiful and we tell them it is their home and to do with the yard what they need in order to make themselves comfortable.

When we go to their homes, to check on the properties they are absolutely gorgeous. The yards are well kept and the interiors are spotless. When you give people the chance to make a home, they are very proud of it.

In our experience, whatever shape the house was in when it was rented is how they keep the house. So, when we rent a house that is absolutely gorgeous, they keep it that way. We've had people in our houses going on six or seven years. That speaks to very satisfied tenants.

Some of our tenants pay their rent two weeks in advance; one tenant pays it a week in advance. Our tenants, for the most part, are never late with their rent payments. We check their homes once a year and they are still beautiful. I marvel how nice they look on the inside. They take such pride in their homes.

We have a lot of houses that have become very happy homes for people.

Make Your Money Up Front

The secret to this business is to make your money up front. You have to know all the numbers before you make an offer on a house. You never get into emotions or anything.

Jim tells us over and over, "The numbers don't lie." And they don't. If the numbers make sense and the house is in a good area for you, then it's a good business step. If the numbers don't make sense, walk away.

Most people who fail in real estate investing pay way too much money for their properties when they buy them. They don't know all the numbers, they just jumped at what they **thought** was a good deal. You never do that.

When we put the offer in on our first flip, we weren't attached to the outcome. If we got it, we got it. If we didn't, the bus always comes around again.

"Blood-sucking Investor"

We've been called things like that and yes, it hurts. One house we looked at was a foreclosure, bank-owned. They were asking $50,000 for it and I offered them $20,000.

That's when they called me a "blood-sucking investor" and I could have gotten upset. But instead, I just laughed and moved on. If the price doesn't work for an investor, they have to be able to move on. What that means to you as a potential investor, have something else you can move toward. At that point in time I had another thirty to forty houses that matched my criteria. This is as Jim taught us to do.

Interestingly enough, that bank called me a few months later and offered the property me for the $20,000 I'd originally offered. At that point, I was too busy with other properties, so I had to turn them down.

It's funny how time changes things. At first I was a "blood-sucking investor," later, I was a potential client.

Even more interesting, a few months later, we bought it for even less than $20,000. We fixed it up and have had people in it ever since.

Try to keep the emotion out of it and you'll have a better business.

Fear Factor

As much as you try to keep emotion out of things, it's not always possible to keep other people's emotions out of it. Whether we're doing flips or rentals, many people are very negative about it.

The first house we bought to rent out, we were doing most of the work ourselves, having our kids help us. Yes, we did this in spite of what Jim taught us. Part of it was we were worried that the negative things people had to say about real estate investing. We thought we'd not hire a contractor the first time out, thinking it might save us some money.

Some of this has to do with fear, and that is something we had to get over. After buying that first house we had people coming out of the woodwork telling us that we were going to lose our shirts. If we believed them, we started feeling afraid...that fear factor coming back.

But the thing is, we already bought it, so we had to make the best of the situation. But, in doing so, we broke one of Jim's rules by trying to do a lot of the work ourselves.

That's the only time we did that. We learned a valuable lesson and we never did it again.

Conquering Self-Doubt

That first house we bought was in another town, a small town that had specific regulations because of the local college up the road. In that town, they have zoning laws that prevent you from renting homes to college kids in certain neighborhoods. We could only rent out to families or other people who were not college kids.

In order to comply, an inspector had to inspect the house to make sure we were complying with their zoning laws. When the zoning officer came to look at the house before we began the rehab work, he took one look at the place and said, "Boy, what a dump. You think you can rent this place out?"

I said, "Of course!"

"You know you can't rent to those college students. You have to rent it out to a single family."

"That's what I want to do," I assured him. "They keep things nicer."

He continued looking through the house. I will admit it was in pretty bad shape. "How much do you think you'll get out of this house?"

I told him we planned on six hundred a month plus utilities. That zoning officer laughed right in my face and said, "I'm telling you, I know this town. This is my town and you'll never get that much."

This was very discouraging news as this was our first rental. We were really counting on that much. In addition, we did our homework and we knew what places were being rented for in the area, so we continued to move forward. I did feel a little apprehensive listening to this local expert who believed that he knew better than I did.

This is where having some training helps because while he was an expert in his town, I'd been trained by an overall real estate expert. That gave me the confidence to continue moving forward.

We got it done and then scheduled to have him return to inspect the house, giving us the OK to rent it now that the rehab was completed.

Now, one of my tricks is about two weeks before the house was done, I put a sign up in front advertising that it is available for rent. We also tell all the neighbors that we'd like to have them come in because after the rehab, the house looks so much better.

The great thing about this tactic is that the neighbors are so impressed with the improvements that they tell everyone they know about this new house that is available for rent.

We signed a lease agreement with an older pair of sisters who thought it was absolutely beautiful. I could hardly wait for the zoning inspector to come in and check out the improvements we had made. We rented it for what I said I wanted, six hundred plus utilities.

The inspector walked into the house and said, "Holy cow! This house looks amazing. It's nicer than my house."

He wrote up the sticker and said we could put it in the window indicating that the house was approved for being rented. Then I told him that I already had people signed up to rent the house for what I wanted.

I was waiting for him to say, "I was wrong."

No, that's not what I got. Instead, he said, "Oh man, I think you could have gotten more."

So much for the guy who "knows this town" and tried to tell me my business.

Don't allow other people to run your business or tear you down. You have to believe in yourself and what you're doing.

Since that time we've also learned that people just like to tell negative stories. Every house that we have bought, neighbors would come out of the woodwork and tell us every bad thing that happened in that house, from storm drain problems to someone dying in a house.

We've gotten to the point now where we would buy a house and then look at each other and ask, "I wonder what story this house has?"

Getting the Neighbors on Your Side

We learned with our first house to get the neighbors involved in what we do. We want them to know that we're not slum lords, so we always invite the entire neighborhood in to look at our completed renovation.

We understand that. They want nice neighbors to move in next door, they don't want a meth lab across the street. It's really interesting, before we have them into the renovated house, we are treated with suspicion and even some hostility. Once they see the completed house, then they like us.

Just don't let people make you fearful.

Jim taught us well. He told us, "This is going to happen to you, and that's going to happen to you." We laugh about that now, but he's right. Knowing what to expect makes you more confident.

Listen to the Right Experts

We learned a lot from Jim. And more importantly, we learned that what Jim told us was the truth. We got a lot of advice from friends, family, neighbors, even perfect strangers who discovered we were getting into real estate investing.

Most of what we have heard from these "nay-sayers" hasn't been true.

Jim has this down to a science. By doing exactly what we learned, we have made money. I have already admitted to not following Jim's advice in the beginning and I lost money because of it. Those several months that I spent rehabbing the house was time rent wasn't coming in.

Make sure you listen to the people who know what they're talking about. Even the zoning inspector wanted to put me down and say I couldn't get the amount of rent I wanted on my first house. But, I had done my homework, and all the numbers said that's what I could charge. In the end, I got exactly what I wanted because I listened to the right people.

How to Evaluate a House

When I look over a house, I go straight to the basement. I know what to look for. The paper that Jim provided in his course is my constant companion. I write down everything I see wrong, and then put in what it's going to cost me. I work my way up from the basement to the attic.

In this way, I can practice rehabbing on paper before I ever commit my own money at it. I know almost exactly how much it is going to cost me.

The way Jim teaches how to do this is so simple anyone, absolutely *anyone* can do it.

Our son was twelve at the time we first started and he wanted to learn what we were doing. So we gave him a checklist and showed him how to use it. He went through a few houses and learned how to use it.

On one of the houses we were considering, we gave our son the checklist, and then had him start in the attic while I started in the basement. We independently evaluated the house and when we compared results, we were within $100 of each other!

If our twelve-year-old son can do this, *anyone* can do this business.

When you learn the process, it takes away the fear and frees you to move forward with confidence.

In one house, I noticed that there wasn't a water meter in the house, and being in town, you have to have a water meter. I noticed that the water line was coming into the house and seemed to come through an empty lot behind the house.

I had my suspicions, so I knocked on the door of the house behind the empty lot and asked them if they knew where the water came from for the house I was considering. They said, "Yes, It comes from our basement." The house I was interested in buying had been owned by the same family, but they had since passed away.

The bank now owned the house and the only way they were going to sell it is if they installed a water meter. That costs money. Most people who want to buy a house aren't interested in installing a water line and water meter before they move in, let alone fix it up and make it livable.

I knew the bank would have a hard time selling that property. AS an investor, I knew exactly how much it was going to cost to get that house rentable. I also know that most investors don't want to deal with a mess with the water company. I told my real estate agent that I wasn't interested, that the bank wanted way too much for that house. I told him that the bank could expect to get $15,000 for that house.

My realtor asked me why I thought it would be such a low price, but I didn't want to reveal what I had discovered. About a year later, the real estate agent called me to see if I might be interested in that property now.

I asked, "Did they put in a new water line?"

"Yes, they did."

What happened is someone put in an offer on the house that the bank accepted. Then the inspector discovered the lack of a water line...and the bank had to install one, at their expense.

This is the beauty of really learning about real estate investing. You recognize problems that seem really huge to people who aren't experienced, and you know they aren't a big deal. You also learn to spot seemingly minor or insignificant problems that can turn into a huge money pit for you. Having to install a water line would have cost me a ton of money and made the property a waste of money for me.

Words of Advice

First, get some training.

Then work with a real estate agent who will listen to your criteria. I tell my real estate agent to go through their MLS for houses that are a particular size and in a particular neighborhood. After I look through those listings, I pare them down to the ones I want to look at.

Then I go through the houses I feel are possibilities and make my list and run my numbers. That way, I know how much a house will be worth once it is fixed up and how much it will cost me to get it to that state.

You'll know the costs for repairs once you work a little bit with your contractor. You'll know how much things will cost, anywhere from painting a room to re-roofing a house. From there, you decide what to do. If the numbers are good, you have a good prospect. If the numbers don't work, you move on to the next house.

There is a bit more to real estate investing than this, but these are the basics. We are very confident in how we do this business because we were trained well and we have proven that it works.

The first time you will be nervous. After you get the first one under your belt, your fear will disappear. Once the fear is gone, there is nothing left but to go up from there!

Part IV

Investment Real Estate is DEAD...as you know it

Ding-dong the witch is dead... In this case; our witch is investment real estate. It's dead. Or at least, it SHOULD be dead but not in the way you think. Now remember my background. I have been an investor for over 27 years and a very large portion of my real estate investment activity has been done the hard way.

The hard way as in actually "doing" the biz.

In case your wondering what that entails it includes the following; driving around looking at properties, touring properties, dealing with real estate agents, dealing with contractors, finding tenants, managing tenants, actually doing rehab work, and on and on and on.

All of those things I did cost me a lot of money to get good at and even once I became good at them, I still didn't like doing it. I just assumed that this was the biz and this is what you did if you wanted to make money investing in real estate.

One day, years ago after asking myself why I was out looking at properties instead of sitting on the beach somewhere it occurred to me. Why should investment real estate be treated any different than any other investment? Meaning, why did it have to be hands on for the investors? Think about it. If you invest in a stock or mutual fund, you are not actively participating; someone is doing it for you. Why not real estate I thought.

I then took it a step further and asked why someone should be investing anywhere but the top markets in the Country? Well, I know WHY they stick to where they live. It's because they don't have the connections or infrastructure to go elsewhere so they invest in an area which may or may not be any good.

Add to the fact that the wealthy make their investments where it makes sense...DOLLARS and Cents! Why should all us regular folks be any different I thought.

Fast-forward to today and it is now a whole new ballgame. You see I learned something from working with thousands of people all over the Country that said they wanted to be real estate investors...they LIED!!! Well, let's say it was a half lie. What they wanted was the RESULTS. They didn't actually want to DO the biz and that reaffirmed everything I thought in the past.

SO these days, we work with investors putting them in the best properties in the best markets in the Country and it is ALL done for them. Their job is to reap the rewards. This is what I meant when I said real estate investment, as you know it is dead. It is dead in the sense that it can be MUCH easier and hands off, and that seems to be what most people want.

This is why most people that buy real estate investment training programs never buy a deal. They want it to be done for them and I am happy to oblige. Below are a few stories from people that agreed with me that the business can and should be much easier and they took advantage of it. This, my friends, is how smart money works.

Case Study – Ken and Teresa Bueller

I always had an interest in real estate and in younger days, after renting for a year or so, thought that renting was just throwing our money away, so at the age of 24, I bought my first house in 1986.

I really liked home ownership as we could work on anything we wanted, could paint any color, put a nail in the wall, and do as we pleased; liked it so much that I wanted to get more properties.

My original dream was to get 12 houses under our belt and back in those days $60K to$75K was the average price for a 3 Br 2Ba home. Unfortunately, I just didn't have the money and didn't know how to get more than one loan as I didn't qualify for anything more than that. I was single and 24 buying my first house with a so-so warehouse job barely qualifying for a $62,000 loan. My job back then simply wasn't enough to fund multiple investment properties.

Actually, I had to sell my 82 Celica Supra as the car payment was too high for me to qualify for my first house. That loan was a 30 year loan with a 9.75% variable APR with a 5% Cap rate meaning it could rise as high as 14.75%, but only increase by 1% per year as I recall. Yikes...

Rates are so much better than those days, we really are super fortunate in this time to be able to buy properties with rates in the 3% to 4% range. That's cheap money, we are blessed today.

So while my dreams back then was to get at least 12 homes that dream never came to fruition, at least yet. I just didn't know how. But the dreams are starting to be realized now thanks to surrounding myself with the right folks, like Jim Toner, his mentors like Frank McKinney, and reading up on what the smart investors did and are doing. Getting around investors I have common interests with. Building the team of smart people to surround myself with has helped us go a lot further. And embracing the Nike saying, Just Do It... If you think about it and don't execute, you'll never get it done...

As time went on, my wife Teresa and I learned a little more about leveraging and using Other People's Money (OPM).

We had a cabin at Tahoe for several years in the family, but just wasn't able to get the family up there regularly enough to justify keeping it and letting it sit idle and unused. So we took a loan out on that and used the proceeds to buy a couple properties in Sacramento. We decided to rent the Tahoe property but eventually sold that for a nice profit.

From that sale, we had enough down payments to purchase two properties in Carmichael, part of Sacramento County, both 3 Br 2 Ba places. Since buying those two properties, they've increased in value significantly to approximately $275K each with us doing nothing more than general fixing up, modest repairs, and finding good tenants and a property management company. But we had a lot to learn still, and still do I suppose.

One of the things we were doing wrong that Jim pointed out was we were putting all of these properties into our own names. Not good from a liability perspective, as well as general credit with the banks and financial institutions. So with Jim's guidance, we opened an LLC and started buying properties into the business. Our first LLC property was out of State in Ohio. This place was fully rented and nets us an additional $500 per month positive cash flow.

Within the same week in September 2014, we bought a fixer-upper property in Sacramento in the Del Paso Heights area. While the property in Sacramento wasn't in the best part of town, we were able to get in at reasonable price, the house had great bones, hardwood floors, and we did a pretty extensive remodel of the property putting it on the market in the spring. This property wasn't just a paint, little landscape, and flip, it required significant rework and some professional assistance from a General Contractor. But we ended up with a pretty healthy profit.

We permitted the work with the county, added an additional bathroom, replacing the roof, and rejuvenating the property with new flooring, paint, granite counters, cabinets, and so on. We did this all along while Ken was working his regular full-time job for the State of California and Teresa was working for the School District. The flip was a fun project but a lot of work too.

The general challenge with Real Estate in Sacramento now-a-days, 2016, is the barriers to entry have increased. It's been getting much pricier in Sacramento to find the killer deals and even so-so deals. Prices are much higher, and deals are fewer and far-between.

However, we've found many of the killer deals still exist and are out of state. But the properties existing out of state is OK, you don't have to live where the properties are if you have good property management support on your team.

I've found actually, that for me, having out of state properties is beneficial as I have this curse of being really handy, and frugal as well. So with the properties in town close to home, I would always find myself over there doing work to one of them which takes up a lot of my time.

With the out of state properties, I am completely hands-off, and the property management companies handle the maintenance leaving me a lot more free time to spend with the family or doing things that I like to do.

Since the Sacramento flip and the one purchase out of state we accumulated another three properties out of state in 2015. Prices were quite reasonable and these are fully rented, all netting each between $500 and $750 per month per house positive cash flow. We're in the process of picking up another property in 2016.

So, while our goal was and still is to accumulate 12 houses, we're 2/3 of the way there already as we have 8 houses today, the majority of which are fully paid off.

While working for the state, we will have a decent pension, at least 40% of our highest salary; however the additional properties as part of our retirement plan will allow us to more comfortably retire with enough additional income to comfortably retire when the time is right.

Getting to 12 properties all yielding us $500 or more each month will easily add another $5,000 to $6,000 per month. But why stop at 12! Think we'll continue to "Just Do It!"

One of the things we're trying to do now is building our Roth and SEP IRA's, to start acquiring some properties into our retirement plans and leverage the benefits of real tax sheltered investing in Real Estate.

We'd like to think we're working a little bit smarter instead of just working harder....

Letting our money actually work for us instead of us working for the money. Jim and his contacts like Edwin Kelley are helping us make that happen.

Good luck to you on your journeys, Jim can help you get to where you want to be...

Case Study – Teresa Ribar

My name is Teresa Ribar and my husband Rick and I live in Queen Creek, Arizona. We attended one of Jim Toners seminars while living in Ohio. At that time, Jim lived in Pennsylvania. We attended a meeting and workshop in Ohio and drove to Pennsylvania a few times for his meetings.

We had attended and even purchased other real estate investing programs. But for some reason or another, we could never make them work. Jim has a program that works if you apply the principles he suggests.

At the workshops and even the introductory meetings we noticed that he was not showing fancy or even lower middle class housing. He was presenting pictures of older homes that had fresh paint and all needed repairs done. They reminded me of one of the homes we rented when we were first married and on a very small budget.

Somewhere that evening, he said "everyone has to live somewhere." Not a rocket science statement but it finally hit us what he was saying. Large, beautiful homes are expensive, not good rentals, and can be risky flips if the numbers are too close to the make or break point. Our primary focus right now is on properties we can hold.

Soon after the seminar and workshop, we made contact with a realtor that quickly found us three homes to purchase. We paid cash for the homes using a checkbook IRA account. (Jim's team goes over the fundamentals in the workshop.) The first home was purchased for $125,000 and rents for $990 per month, the second for $116,000 and rented for $900 per month and the third was a condominium for $69,000 bringing in $690 per month. That totals $2,580 per month before expenses (tax, insurance HOA fees management fees, and any needed repairs). We thought we were doing really well for ourselves.

Almost a year after we purchased the properties we discovered that the realtor was less than honest with us as well as some very major investors. To make a long a painful story short, she is now serving twelve years in prison. You may take that as your first lesson. Always check out the people you are giving your hard earned money too.

Rick and I felt horrible. We had been taken. We needed advise and turned to Jim. He helped us pick up our pride and get back to business. He asked questions about the purchases, what we paid, location, etc. He called me back to tell us he had checked out our purchases and they were growing in value and long term we would be okay. He then told us that by selling those properties and reinvesting in some older homes in the Akron Ohio area, he felt we could make more money and recover our loses much faster.

We had enough cash to purchase two of these homes, each at $35,000. There was no realtor involved, only the seller and the title company. Closing costs were less than $500. We were given the address which we looked up on GoogleMaps and Zillow. We were able to see the outside of the home and the neighborhood. Not a pretty neighborhood or home, but it was clean, in a good location, in good repair, and was affordable. We referred it as our throw away house. Meaning that if it didn't work out, we could dump it quickly and cheap.

Both houses rent for $550 per month before expenses. There are no HOA fees in this neighborhood (the seller is also the management company). The management company keeps the first month's rent for any needed repairs throughout the year, plus 10% of the monthly rent as their fee. I thought it was a little high but they said that we would not be getting bills throughout the year for minor repairs. We have never received a repair bill to date.

So now we are getting $550 a month X two units. That is $1100 per month before expenses. But our investment was only $70,500, which is closest to the cost of the single condo unit we purchased. Woohoo!

So we purchased a third house as soon as we could scrap together the money. Now we have three single homes at $35,000 each and renting for $1650 per month before expenses. Now we can see the benefit. And it didn't take very long to fall in love with the monthly checks.

The management company is literally doing EVERYTHING. They drive though the neighborhoods all the time. The tenets love them because they are quick to fix what is broken. They collect the rent, write the check and I make a deposit.

We are currently rehabbing the house that we purchased for $116,000. It will be listed for $135,000 or better and our new and more ethical realtor expects it to sell quickly. We expect to clear our costs but not make a huge profit on this house. Once sold, we will immediately purchase as many homes as we can with the proceeds. Obviously we are hoping to purchase three more of the homes in Akron with the funds. That doubles our current income on those houses.

It should work out mathematically like this:

Three existing homes purchased at $35000 each, all with closing costs less than $500. Total: $106,500.00

Rent on three homes at $550 each (one of them rents for $590) equals $1650 less 10% maintenance fees to total $1485.00 per month, which is what we deposit every month.

Purchase at least three more houses (from the proceeds of the one rental) to double our holdings and we deposit $2970 per month. Which is more than the $2580 per month we received (before expenses) for the three homes in Arizona. We are in the process of purchasing a fourth house now with the funds from all combined rentals. Because it is an IRA account we are able to continue to re-invest our proceeds to build for our retirement.

We are permitted two trips per year to check on those investments. We have family in Ohio that we visit while there which is a bonus (and a tax write-off as well).

As the other renters leave the properties we own in Arizona, we plan to sell them and reinvest where it makes sense to do so. I no longer care if it is in Ohio, Pennsylvania or Alaska. Jim does his homework, he crunches the numbers and if the numbers don't work and the people are not honest, he walks away. I respect his choices and am very happy to be a part of his real estate family.

Best of Luck to you.

Case Study – Russell Lewis

Investing in properties in an area in which you do not live is not an easy thing to consider for most people and it was the same for me. There are many things that concerned me initially but that all changed once I saw all the facts.

My initial concern was not being able to see the actual property in person to do a walk thru. To many people, that would be like buying a pig in a sack. Another concern was not being able to monitor what was really going on at the property. On the top of my list was – "Will I be able to get my rent money".

There is no doubt that these were the 3 top reasons that were in my mind when I first considered investing in the 3 "Cash Flow" properties I now own in Ohio. By the way, I live in Sacramento CA.

What really gave me the confidence to invest in the "cash flow" deals was Jim Toner. He kept reiterating, "Buy where the deals are" and "Live where you want and BUY where it makes sense...Dollars and Cents" With Jim leading the way, it was Ohio.

Jim had continually let the people in his Creating Wealth 101 program know that the economy was in grave danger and the 2016 downward slide on the stock market proved him to be true.

Thank goodness I had already decided to close out my stocks and IRA'S and use the money to invest in out of State, Cash Flow properties with Jim leading the way.

Jim always preached that investment real estate can be no different than any other investment as far as a person's involvement. Jim always says that it CAN and SHOULD be all done for you and he is right.

My properties are all taken care of and are hands off for me. Now I am receiving double-digit returns on a REAL investment as opposed to my money floating around in the Stock Market.

I would encourage everyone to become educated in the area of Cash Flow properties and if you live in an area where home prices are too high...by ALL means, look into States where it makes sense.

Russell Lewis, Sacramento CA

Case Study – Robert Sommer

October 2014 I was unemployed after 30 years working for a Pittsburgh Advertising and Marketing company that had merged with a competitor. Unemployed not by my own choice for the first time in my life, I now had full control and access to my 401k money and was in need of somewhere to invest it. Not a big fan and suspicious of the present stock market I contacted Jim Toner and told him my situation.

I met Jim when he lived in Pittsburgh as one of his students and was very interested in investment real estate because it made more sense to me as a safer investment than the uncertainties of the stock market and other investments. Also, In the past I had lost a lot of money real fast in a non-real estate investment.

With Jim's help he guided me to a couple of very serious real estate investors with lots of experience who had many rental properties in Akron, Ohio that were rehabbed, occupied and manage by them. They also advised me on how to transfer my 401k funds to a self directed IRA.

I was concerned about buying real estate investment properties out of state, but I didn't know anyone in Pittsburgh that I could trust that could help me invest in Pittsburgh.

Akron, Ohio is only a couple hours away from Pittsburgh, so I drove to Akron and met with Jim's investor friends and took a tour of the Akron rental real estate market. I was impressed by the investors, the houses, the neighborhoods and how the numbers worked and decided to buy one. Then I bought 3 more. I printed, signed, scanned and emailed all the closing forms from The Carnegie Library in the West End of Pittsburgh.

Now as I watch the up and downs of the stock market going down more than up, I am glad that I invested in real estate and can see my self-directed IRA growing every month with the rental checks.

Part V

The Curtain

"Never underestimate the ignorance of the general public"

P.T. Barnum

Ouch, that hurts. You gotta admit that is a pretty strong statement coming from old P.T.....but...the truth is not always kind now is it?

People are believers or at least we WANT to believe. We have a habit, a bad one, of seeing things not as they ARE, but instead, how we WANT them to be.

Hey, I get it; I catch myself falling into this from time to time also. However, as the business years pass I have become VERY adept at sniffing out bullshit before it gets to my doorstep.

And this brings me to the Curtain. Now the Curtain, depending on which side of it you are on can be good, or bad. So, what IS the Curtain?

By the way, before I let you in on this, you need to understand that I am divulging "secrets" used by all who are in the position of "expert" or as us insiders say....the WIZARDS! This chapter may also piss of anyone in the industry who happens to read it. Too bad.

So, back to the Curtain. The Curtain is the invisible barrier between you and me. You see on MY side of the Curtain I have magic powers that will boggle the mind. I have the secrets of the ages. I have the answers and cures to all that ales you.

I…am the Wizard, and Wizards have power. Some use it for good, others, not so much. More on that later.

Now, on YOUR side of the Curtain…well now that can be a dangerous place to be. The reason is because when you are on YOUR side, you carry with you the hopes and dreams that you are praying the person on the other side can fulfill.

All your problems and worries can be dissolved by the Wizard on the other side with a simple wave of the wand. But what is the danger you may be wondering? Well, the danger is that on the other side, the Wizard may or may not be an evil Wizard, or worse yet, he or she may not even be a Wizard at all!

And the biggest danger of all in this drama is that it will most likely cost you LOTS of money to find out the truth of the Wizard.

Feeling like you're in Alice in Wonderland yet? Stick with me.

So let's talk about the Wizards. We will start with me. Am I a Wizard? Of course I am, what else would you expect me to say? Seriously, I am. I do have secrets, and tools and tricks that can and will turn your life around if properly applied. I am also, a "good" Wizard. I will do the very best I can for anyone that is putting their faith and money in me.

On the down side, if that is how you would view it is I am VERY blunt...sometimes, painfully so. I know the aforementioned quote by P.T. Barnum is unfortunately true.

The vast majority of the general public tends to be sheep that are more than willing to be herded in any direction dictated by whatever dictator is dictating to them. How's that for a cool sentence?

Sorry, I digress. As I was saying, I am blunt when I am working with someone one that has hired my services. I am blunt for a few reasons. The first being I have found NOT being blunt tends to run the risk of having the message NOT sink in.

Here is an example: One of the questions I get from those looking to make money by investing in real estate is. "Does this really work?" My answer is, "Yes, IF you do as I say and follow thru. If you do not, I guarantee you will NOT make any money"

Now see, most if not all gurus would avoid a comment like that like because it plants the seed of doubt. They want no part of it. They NEVER would tell you that you won't make money. Why? Because that would shatter the illusion. That would remove their hand from your wallet.

I operate in the opposite fashion. If I can't help you or think you will not participate in helping yourself, sorry, I'm not going to play. The hassle you will cause me is not worth any fees I charge. I have and DO fire clients and customers.

I WANT you to succeed because that helps both of us. Because I want you to succeed I do things that will set up that success. I will be blunt, tell you the truth, and not gouge you on fees and so forth.

The "other Wizards" on the other hand...let's just say the VAST majority, and I mean almost ALL of them, will be pretty angry that I am revealing this. For anyone thinking I am throwing them under the bus because they are competition, you would be wrong. I have no competition. Lots of guys doing it, very little competition.

I am very specific on who and how many I work with which gives me a very big advantage over the fools I will discuss now. I simply believe in TELLING THE TRUTH!!!!! If someone is coming to you with their hopes and dreams and hard earned money you damn well better take it very seriously and deliver. Sadly, more often than not, it doesn't happen. So here you go.

WELCOME TO THE "HOW TO GET RICH IN REAL ESTATE SEMINAR"

Feel free to insert any name of most any "guru" in with the above sentence being that they are all pretty much the same. I want to walk you thru the world and "systems" of the "make money in real estate" space.

First let me say that YES, you can absolutely get rich investing in real estate. No doubt! I did, as have possibly millions of others. That is the good news. Now, for the bad news...10x more did not and most that attend these seminars will not.

Before you get too discouraged let's remember that "Rich" is a relative term. For some people if they make $100,000 a year, they are rich. For others, it needs to be a million. You get the point. However, what if you got involved in investment real estate and only made an additional $50,000 a year? Would that be so bad? How about if you were able to turn the returns going into your retirement accounts into 10% - 15% instead of ZERO or worse. Would that be so bad? No, it would actually be pretty great. I will show you how to do that in a later chapter by the way.

Moving into this, let's look at things from that prospective because the likelihood of you becoming a millionaire from a get rich in real estate seminar is VERY slim. You can however, make yourself a VERY nice additional income and eventually live off of your investments or quit your job or both.

What will greatly increase your likelihood of success is getting off on the right foot and having what I like to call, "Eyes Wide Open".

If you are wondering WHOM in particular I am talking about here you can just assume it is just about EVERY guru. I know the inside secrets in the industry as well as the people and it's not too pretty. But, it is what it is. So here is the formula.

It starts with the advertising. When said "guru" is coming to your town you will hear ad's on the radio nonstop for about 2 weeks telling you that YOUR TOWN is the BEST place in the County to make money in real estate. That's the first lie.

All real estate is LOCAL and there are MANY areas you should not be investing in depending on the economic climate. You will also be led to believe that the "main" guru" will also be at the "Free" event. That's the next lie. It is important to create a "cult of personality". People want to meet the "famous" "successful guy" This is a very powerful tool. One of the Guru's bases his entire business on this strategy.

The above by the way applies to all the infomercial gurus as well as the guys sending you the direct mail pieces. Some of them do all of that. It's pretty good marketing actually but it is VERY expensive marketing. Someone needs to pay for that. Any guess who?

So the radio ads or infomercial or mailer have hooked you with the promise of you being in the right place at the right time and now the right guy is coming to town to save you. All you need to do is show up at one of the FREE seminars being held in the coming weeks.

Nothing wrong with that, FREE seminar. Most will offer a Free gift for attending.

At the seminar, which is very carefully choreographed, you will most likely be shocked when "the guy" is not there but instead, one of his associates. To be fair, most of these "gurus" do disclose, in very fine print or fast-talk that the "guy" will not be there in person. Most however don't catch it due to the nature of the ad leads you to believe they will be there.

The associate however will waste no time telling you how awesome he himself is, or she, and they will begin with the bag of tricks that are frankly so old I really can't believe people fall for it.

I don't want to go step by step what happens the entire time as it will take to long. The bottom line is this, they are VERY short on any REAL content and VERY heavy on motivation and what I call "bait".

The goal is to entice as many in the crowd as possible to attend what is most likely going to be a 2 or 3 day event in which ALL secrets will be revealed and you will be on your way to Real Estate Riches. To make this even more appealing the cost to attend is very low, $1,000 and under. Some even go as low as a few hundred bucks. This entire "show" is designed to get you into the weekend event, not to teach you how to invest in real estate as you were led to believe.

For those who chose to attend the 2 or 3 day training what you will be receiving is very likely a few strategies that you can apply and make some money, which is good right? That's what you paid for.

Not likely because the majority of the time however, you will be puffed up with motivation and primed for upsells. That means...getting the BIG money out of you. The reason they do this is because if they told you the truth at the FREE seminar, the weekend program would consist of a few strategies and A LOT of up-selling to a higher priced program, not many would bite.

In full disclosure, I have no problem at all how much someone charges for their products of services.

Frankly, I am very well compensated by those I work with. I like to call it, "Reassuringly Expensive".

My problem is not what is charged, but HOW it is gone about and WHAT is delivered. If you want to charge someone $100,000 for coaching I'm fine with that as long as you DELIVER on that. I know many will say that if someone decides to buy something that is their decision. I get it, it is what it is and I don't want to get into the morality of the issue, I'm just pointing out my thoughts as someone that has been in the game longer than most as well as point out how this system works and the dangers of it.

You see, during these weekends, the goal is to ALWAYS get more money from the participants. Now you start moving into the $10,000 and up range. One VERY well known group actually has attendees at their weekend event do the "homework" assignment of getting their credit card limit raised. Any guess why?

Some sign people up to go on "Bus Tours" where you pay anywhere to $25,000-$40,000 to get on a bus and look at homes with your favorite guru. Please re-read that line...to LOOK AT HOMES!

Listen, these Companies and I say Companies because most of the "guru's " are simply a front person hired by the real owners who are people you will never see or most likely even know about, but nonetheless, their goal is to make big money. I get it, and I agree with it. What I don't agree with is how it is done.

Some think it is ok to operate like this and maybe I'm wrong but if you are someone that wants to spend

$40,000 to go "look" at properties, you for sure are not my client. But hey, whatever floats your boat. Just remember, you have been warned.

I saved the 2 biggest problems with the guru's for last and they are problems.

The first is this. Even though many of these Companies have good training and do deliver some solid information, that is, IF, you pay the big money, the big problem is ongoing support or, a big lack thereof. It has been my experience, and I have been at this 27 years, that unless you have access to someone better that is available to help you, there is a very good chance you will fail.

You can give someone the greatest information in the world but once they are left on their own, things can go sideways. You need to have access to a REAL mentor, not a salesperson from a support line. I have had many mentors that got me thru the real estate investment jungle and that is the only reason I made it. You need one also. Are there those who can succeed without it? Sure, but they are rare. Like my dad used to say, "even a blind pig roots up an ear of corn every once in a while"

The final problem is the biggest of all. INTEGRETY, or should I say, LACK of.

Remember back in the beginning I talked about the Wizard behind the curtain? Remember in Oz when the Wizard was exposed he wasn't all he was cracked up to be? Same here only worse. If you knew the REAL story of many of these people you would NEVER go within 100 miles of them let alone listen to them.

When you have to PAY fees to online ratings sites to stop people from complaining about your company... you are bad. Sorry, you are BAD.

There is a very well known so called "consumer protection" site out there that I will not dignify by naming because they are nothing but an extortion site. This is a site people can go to if they feel they have been wronged by a Company. When someone checks your company out, they find this site if someone complained with them. By the way, I'm not referring to the BBB.

Let me ask you. Do you think it is a problem that the "guru's" PAY this site monthly fees to quite the unhappy customers quiet? Here is how the sick game works... said site, is operated by a former convicted felon and con artist but the general public thinks it is a site to help protect consumers and that this con is their advocate.

If a customer has been wronged, they go to this site and file a complaint, which shows up on the first page of Google. The guru finds out about the complaints and contacts the site and is told, "Nope, we never take complaints down, UNLESS you pay us a monthly FEE and we will say that we investigated and you are approved".

The con that runs the company is operation could care less about any one actually filing the complaint because he is only concerned about extorting fees from people that want the complaints to stop. Like I said...pretty sick

So now the Gurus pay because they want to keep the image that NO ONE ever complains and they are super awesome. Now I don't know about you and I for sure am not telling anyone how to live their lives but if you don't see a very big problem with what I described, we are not compatible.

The integrity is gone and it's now only about the money. That my friends, is what is behind the curtain of MOST EVERY guru out there. They may have started with good intentions....

So, can you get rich in real estate? Sure, but there are easier, far less expensive ways than giving your hard earned cash to anyone that operates like that.

In case you may have missed to basic math issue here, I will point it out. If you spend $20,000 - $40,000 to go on BUS TOURS...where does that leave you financially?

Do you realize there are parts of the Country that you can have deals that are DONE FOR YOU, with purchase prices of $30,000-$40,000, fully rehabbed, rented and managed that return up to 15%? Is it a wiser move to do that or ride a bus and look at houses?

I'm just asking. It's your money and you can certainly do what you want with it. As a matter of fact, there are people out there that are perpetual learners that take program after program and never do anything else. Some people actually like that. But then there are the rest that actually want to get a positive result and when it comes to that, you need to make smart business decisions.

For years I have taught thousands throughout the Country how just 12 little properties can give you a new worth of over 2 Million Dollars and over $100,000 a year in income. Now I know that won't put you on the Forbes list but it is for sure nothing to shake a stick at.

Look at the stories in this book from those who did what I taught them and look at the results. By the way, they did it during the real estate down turn. Now look at those doing it today with "Done For You" programs.

The bottom line on both is results.... as in, getting them.

So there is light at the end of the tunnel. It can either be the rainbow at the pot of gold, or, it can be the light of an oncoming train. The path you take will decide which one.

F*K The Demons Of Doubt

By John Mulry

I doubt myself.

Every. Single. Day.

There. I said it.

Even though I'm a bona fide, marketing maverick that can absolutely transform your business and your life I doubt myself and I think it's killing me.

Or at least I thought I did.

I'm my own worst critic. There's an internal dialogue or battle rather going on in my head constantly - questioning everything I do, questioning what I've done...

Things like...

My books *The Truth!* And *Your Elephants Under Threat* which although have received worldwide recognition and have already helped countless businesses and people I doubt myself for writing them and for selling them...

I doubt whether they are any good. I doubt whether people should buy them. I doubt anyone will read them and get anything from them.

And I doubt whether you will read this. I doubt whether you will enjoy it. I doubt whether or not it will help you.

I also doubt my other products and services. I doubt my referral system. I doubt my lost customer reactivation system. I doubt my online business launch system. I doubt my local business software system. I doubt my done with you and done for you programs.

As fantastic as all those things are - I on occasion doubt any and all of them because of the battle inside my head. I doubt, I question, I second guess, I over analyse and I fall into a cycle of hatred and loneliness.

At this time of writing I'm going through hell and back personally which makes me doubt absolutely EVERYTHING.

Even more.

I mean if it's all this hard, what's the point. Why go on? Why bother right? Well there is a point and there is ALWAYS reason to go on. Always.

All the while I'm doubting myself and everything I do to help you succeed all I think of is the demons of doubt who are choking me, squeezing every bit of optimism and hope out me waiting for me to crumble. All of this is going on and I feel alone. Feel like I'm the only one who's like this. Feeling like a fraud. A failure. A nobody.

Being hit with a bombshell that crushes you breaks even the strongest of wills.

But then something happens. Maybe not immediately but it happens. And it can from nowhere, come from someone or something that you had all along. For me it was a couple of well written words from a book that changed everything.

"Start asking the right questions not the wrong ones."

Instead of *"Why can't I?"* ask *"How can I?"*

So I did. And I am. And the doubt is fading. Not gone but fading.

And I understand now. Doubt is part of the journey. Without doubt there's no progress. Doubt means we're heading into the discomfort zone which is where the success comes. Not the comfort zone. That's where mediocrity lives.

F*k mediocrity.

Without doubt - however ugly and uncomfortable it is - there would be no winning. Everybody doubts themselves and it took a great book for me to understand that.

If you're doubting what you're doing, the direction you're going, the validity of your ideas, whether you're good enough to be in investment real estate, whether you're worthy, whether you deserve it - I want you to know that you're not alone.

I'm beside you - doubting too. But I'm not giving up. And neither should you. I am a doubter. But I'm also a fighter. And I'm fighting. And I'm also a winner. And I'm winning.

I'm doubting but I'm fighting. For what I want. To fulfill MY mission. Of seeing just how much of my potential I can achieve. To push myself to my limit. To see how far I can go and to help others go far too.

Best of all. I'm barely in first gear at the minute. I'm just lifting my foot off the clutch. There's a long way to go. And there'll be more doubts. With more success comes more challenges. So I'm a doubter and you probably are too. That's ok. Because we're not alone.

The best of the best all doubt themselves.

Every. Damn. Day.

And the ones who say they don't are liars. And the biggest doubters of them all. But they fight too. As clichéd as it is and it's been said a million times before. It isn't about getting hit; it's about getting up when you get hit.

I've been knocked out. But I'm awake now. And I'm fighting back. And I'll win.

You should too.

Keep striving. Keep doubting. But keep fighting. If you want to achieve something exceptional, "normal" just doesn't cut it. Don't be normal.

Remember to ask yourself the right questions not wrong ones. Next time you doubt yourself ask these questions:

- What can I learn from this, which will make me stronger?
- What can I do differently next time?
- How can I improve?
- Can this experience help me refine my game plan, or help me identify skills that I need to work on?

Jim has given you the roadmap to success with investment real estate. You've read his story; you can grasp his methods like countless others have – now it's your time.

When you begin and work towards your first deal or your first house you'll have doubts – don't let them hold you back. Ask those questions. Consult this book. Consult with Jim. Use his support system. Use his systems. Use his mentoring. Remember doubting whether you can do it or whether or not you're good enough is part of the process.

At this moment you're excited – that's brilliant but you're also scared. That's also brilliant. Being scared means you want it. Being scared and doubting whether or not you can ACTUALLY achieve financial freedom through investment real estate is normal. It's outside your comfort zone. But you can. Just stick to the plan

Jim has given you in this book. It works. Just look at all his case studies.

Remember you're not alone. You have Jim. You have his support. All you have to do is ask for it. He can help you but more importantly he WANTS to help you. You've read the book – you're excited and scared but all you have to do now is take the first step forward – everything else will fall into place. Go forward and expect success.

JM

Why Work With Us

For those of you who work with me, you'll get the benefit of everything I've learned over the past twenty-seven years. I have done so many deals, so many different *kinds* of deals, and you can't put a price on that kind of experience.

I don't teach theory.

I don't teach fluff.

I don't teach "filler" material.

I teach real world applications in real estate investing, both the good and the bad. I've lost money, heck, I've lost a ton of money. Most people in real estate investing have lost money.

But that's what happens when you don't know what you're doing.

What Mentorship Does

Working with a mentor helps you to move forward. Before I started in real estate investing, I studied just about every book and program I could get my hands on.

The problem was that I was afraid.

- I was afraid of what I didn't know.
- I was afraid of what might happen.
- I was afraid of the unknown.

The instant I started working with the guy I had chosen as my mentor, I discovered that I actually knew more about real estate investing than my mentor did. What working with my mentor accomplished was it took away my fear.

Mentorship gives you the confidence you need to move forward with a project, or the courage to back away from a deal you initially thought was good, but then turned bad on you.

Working with a mentor also helps you to avoid pitfalls that can cost you a ton of money. Hopefully from the Case Studies we have provided, you have learned from the experiences of others how having a mentor saved them from making some very expensive mistakes.

Just a couple of mistakes in this business can put you out of business. Hiring a mentor is more than worth the money you will save. With our program, you can call us anytime about anything. It never expires.

Avoiding Costly Mistakes

As you learned from my story, I made plenty of mistakes in the beginning of my real estate investing career. On a deal where I should have cleared about $30,000, I only cleared $17,000 because I didn't know how to deal with the various professionals I would be working with.

By working with me, we teach our clients how to become experts at dealing with contractors: the questions to ask, the contracts to use with them, and how they should perform in order to make you money.

We also teach you how to find a decent attorney, one who is interested in developing a relationship with you. Not one who just wants to make money off you.

You've heard from a number of our students that you have to work with the right kind of real estate agent, one who is experienced at working with investors. Having the right agent will save you a ton of time and a ton of money.

I learned the hard way that you can't take anyone's word for anything. We teach you how to make your experts prove that they will do what they say they're going to do, and this is going to save you big time on every deal.

What is critical to understand about real estate investing is you must make your money when you buy. When you work a deal that might bring in $5,000 and you make mistakes...you could end with not very much money. Or, worse, you could end up owing money. Say you made two $3,000 mistakes? You'd end up owing $1,000 by the time you were done with your project.

However, if you make sure you make your money on the purchase and the deal you just got could net you $25,000 and you still made those two $3,000 mistakes, you'd still end up making $19,000.

With me, you will learn how to buy your properties at the right price so that if you do make mistakes, you will still make a profit. And at the end of the day, making money is why you're interested in real estate investing, isn't it?

Part VI

Philanthropy: The Key to Success is Giving Back

The Universal Law

Some people get this, and others don't, but one of the tricks to accumulating wealth is to give things away. It's just the way it is. When you give, you get back, but not necessarily from the person you gave it to.

We've all fallen on hard times. I've had times when I've been down so far I was afraid that I wouldn't be able to dig myself out, and then out of the blue, something would happen that would help me to get out of it. I can only attribute that to the charity work I've always done.

I was reading the paper one day and there was a story about homeless veterans. The article said that one out of every four homeless people is a veteran. That really bothered me. My dad was a World War II veteran and it seemed like vets were treated differently back then. Now it seems as if veterans are "disposable" and that doesn't make sense to me.

What could I do? I wanted to make a statement, take a stand against this kind of apathy toward our veterans.

My expertise is in real estate investments. I decided to take a property, totally rehab it, and turn it into a brand new house. I intended to give it away totally free to a veteran who was just coming home.

We had a lot of people sending in entries, but the one that really caught my attention was from a lady who sent an entry in for her brother who was still over in Iraq doing his fourth tour of duty. While he was over there his wife hooked up with another guy who wound up murdering their daughter.

We awarded that veteran a totally refurbished home. He took me aside afterward and said, "You need to understand, I would be homeless if it weren't for what you have done."

Here was a vet who had put his life on the line, getting injured, and suffering from PTSD. When I thought about my own problems, they seemed pretty insignificant compared to this guy. He couldn't believe what we had done. It virtually turned his life around.

Everyone needs to understand the impact that they have. You don't have to give a house away. You can volunteer your time and your talent. You can give something back.

The Caring House Project Foundation

You've heard talk about the Caring House Project Foundation from a few of our students in the Case Histories section of this book. I want to take a few more minutes of your time and really emphasize just how important it is to give back with your Time, Talent, and Treasure.

When we are as fortunate as we are to be successful in investment real estate, we can do some really wonderful things for others.

Nothing is worthwhile until you give back.

The Real Value of Real Estate

Being involved in investment real estate has made my life absolutely wonderful. At one point in my life I was really doing well in this industry, making a lot of money, taking month-long vacations, living in a beautiful home, driving the car of my dreams.

I was down in Florida on one of my month-long vacations and happened to be wandering around in a book store when a book caught my eye. It was the book *Make it Big* by Frank McKinney.

I had never heard of this guy, but looking at the front of the book I was looking at a guy who looked like a rock star and I'll admit, I was really intrigued. Flipping through the pages, I began to compare myself to him, saying, "I did that...I did that...no big deal, I did that..."

Then I turned another page and said, "Whoa! I *didn't* do that! I *didn't* do this!"

Now this guy had my attention. I bought the book, took it home and started reading it. I was crazy impressed, not so much with his real estate activities, which *are* beyond incredible because he went from doing $40,000 junker homes to fifty million dollar homes.

That's a quantum leap by anyone's standard.

What really impressed me was what Frank McKinney was doing on the philanthropic side of his life. What he was doing with all the money he was making.

He was giving back to the world, not just his community, and *that* got my attention.

Right about that time we were trying to start a charitable foundation, but didn't know anything about it, how to start it, how to set up, etc. I had worked with the Salvation Army for many years, but I was looking for something that gave more directly to the people who needed it.

My idea was to collect money and then donate it to people who really needed it. But, I didn't know how to go about doing that.

In Frank's book, I discovered that he volunteers at a place called the Caring Kitchen in Del Rey, Florida and I was just blown away that a guy who went from just a beginning real estate investor to being the best in the world is so interested in giving back.

Giving back is a huge part of his life and that of his wife, Nilsa.

I figured that Frank McKinney might just be the guy I needed to talk to. But, I also knew that the likelihood of actually talking to this man was pretty slim. Regardless, I tracked down a phone number for the Caring Kitchen and said, "I would like to talk to this guy named Frank McKinney who works down there."

The voice on the phone sounded very pleasant, "Oh, Mr. McKinney, absolutely. Let me take your name and number and he'll get back to you."

Right. I'd heard that before. Still, I left my information but I will admit right now that I never expected, *ever*, to hear from him.

Within a couple of hours the phone rings and I'm talking to the rock star of real estate himself. We hit it off right away and as I explained what I wanted to do, Frank was very interested in helping me get started. He told me a couple years later that he has had a number of people call him for the same kind of information, but they never followed through. He told me that I was the first guy who ever did.

Anyway, Frank explained how to set up the charitable foundation, and from that point we became friends. As I got to know Frank more and more, he became a mentor to me, not for real estate, but on the philanthropic side.

I was tremendously influenced by everything he did on the side. My interest in charitable causes and philanthropy didn't begin with Frank, but getting to know him really expanded my understanding of the potential I had to make positive changes in people's lives.

Prior to this I had given away some homes. The first time I did it, I gave it to a veteran who had returned from the war. It was a big deal, covered by the paper and national news. Frank heard about it and was impressed, which let me know I was on the right track. "Man, that was really great how you did that. I'm proud of you."

My interest in philanthropic activities came about as a result of reading personal development books. I've read pretty much every book there is to read about real estate investing. But I knew I wanted to improve myself as a person, and in just about every book there was a section on how you need to give back to others in your community.

Before too long, philanthropy became a way of life.

As a result of our friendship, Frank asked me to serve on his board of directors for his charitable foundation, The Caring House Foundation. He and his wife, Nilsa, started this foundation to help the people of the world.

The scope of the work concentrates mainly on Haiti. What many people don't realize is that Haiti is the poorest country in the Western hemisphere. It has the dubious honor of the highest infant mortality rate of children under five in the world, and the average life expectancy for adults is about 48 years old.

Frank feels that while we are doing things here in the U.S., there are safety nets here. No matter how bad things are, there are usually safety nets of some kind.

Over there, there are no safety nets. Haiti is a mere hour and a half airplane ride from this country, and yet it is like an entirely different world.

What Caring House Foundation does over there is build self-sustaining villages.

This is truly an appealing concept. Frank's a big believer in not just giving people something, but build something that will have a lasting impact. The idea of the self-sustaining villages with renewable food sources, renewable water sources is not just giving those people something to last them a week. It actually creates a culture for them where they can support themselves.

Being involved in The Caring House Foundation has been a life-changing experience.

Imagine, instead of giving people just a turkey, you give them animal husbandry skills where they are taught how to raise animals for food, always with an eye for tomorrow's food.

My first experience in Haiti was when I went with Frank and about ten other people. In order to land, the pilot had to buzz the runway to get the cows to move off the runway so we could land. Getting off the plan was surreal because there were armed guards holding machine guns.

We met up with an organization called Food for the Poor, our ground contact in Haiti. They took us on a tour to show us how bad things were there. I don't recall the name of the place, but I think it was the Swamps…what a nightmare! I will never forget what that place looked like. It was sewage mixed with landfill into a gray muck, and in the middle of all this were kids just sitting in this stuff.

Most of the people didn't have houses, and the ones who did lived in corrugated tin shacks.

This tour gave us visible evidence of the incredible need in Haiti. Most people don't really believe that people live like this.

From there, we toured the self-sustaining villages created by the Caring House Foundation. One of the biggest problems in Haiti is that most buildings are just slapped together, and when the earthquake hit, everything fell down.

The homes we built did not collapse. They all withstood the earthquake. A solid home for four people costs $2,500. For a little less than $5,000 we can build homes that will house eight people.

Do you know what a major deal it is for people who have been living in shacks or in the dirt? To have a solid, virtually indestructible home changes their lives.

By using our real estate investment knowledge and our business acumen, money-making skills, and fund-raising skills, we can apply all of this to make a massive impact on the country of Haiti and is exactly what we are doing.

The villages we build include a community center, schools, housing, animal husbandry, tilapia ponds...virtually everything a village would need in order to survive on its own.

All of this was Frank McKinney's brain-child and I'm more than happy to help him. I want to make an impact there, make a difference in the world. On a recent visit there we visited one of the villages we had completed and it was absolutely thriving! They appreciated what we provided, they took advantage of it and took it over and made it work for them.

At my workshops, I always make sure that I show people what $3,500 can do to make a difference in the world. With that kind of donation, you impact the lives of four people. Do that a couple more times and you've impacted the lives of that many more people.

Frank's website, www.Frank-McKinney.com will take you right to his website and there you can read all about his Caring House. There are so many ways to donate, you can donate anywhere from ten dollars a month to $175,000 to create an entire village that will build fifty homes and care for over four hundred people.

Everyone can do something and that has been our focus in Haiti. We were there long before the earthquake, and we will be there long afterward.

Had it not been for investment real estate, I would have never been able to be involved in such an amazing program. Even more wonderful is how many people

I've met who are real estate investors who also want to be involved in the Caring House Foundation.

I have a whole bunch of my clients and students who are now involved with and supporting Caring House with their Time, Talent, and Treasure.

Some of my greatest business contacts and best friends have come from my connections through Caring House.

The reason I met Frank McKinney had absolutely nothing to do with real estate. When I look back on it, it never occurred to me to ask him questions about investment real estate; I wanted to pick his brain about setting up a charitable foundation.

What really drew me to Frank was the caring and loving way he embraced Haiti and decided to build his foundation to help the Haitian people.

My wife and I were able to build a community center down there and I wouldn't have been able to do anything like that if I weren't a real estate investor.

In fact, none of my life would have been possible if I had followed the same plan that so many people have followed, "Go to school, get a good job, keep your nose to the grindstone, and everything will work out."

It didn't work for me twenty-five years ago, and I'm delighted because I'm loving the life I live today. Even more important than the life I live is the change that I can make in the world by working with Frank and the Caring House Foundation for the people of Haiti.

When I talk to people about real estate, I say, "Listen, here's the goal: make enough money so you can have an awesome lifestyle, nice car, nice house, nice vacation...then make enough so that you can do that all for your family and then for a few more people, and then the real goal is to take care of as many people as you can.

How cool would it be if you could take care of ten, twenty, or a hundred people that you don't even know?

That's what it's all about.

That's the message we provide at our workshops, that's why you want to get into this business.

You'll make plenty of money for yourself and that will be awesome.

But, to really make an impact, start doing some cool stuff for other people and that's the whole thing about investment real estate for me. It affords that income to make a difference for others.

Part VII

Appendix

TERMS

ADA – Americans with Disabilities Act.

Appraisal – The value put on a piece of property by a professional.

Appreciation – An increase in the value of an asset/property over time.

ARV – After Repair Value

Asset – Something of value that you own.

Collateral – A valuable asset used as security for a loan.

Comps (Comparables) – Comparable real estate transactions that have taken place in the same neighborhood in the same time frame and for a similar property. Prices are established by using comps.

Default – Failing to fulfill a legal obligation or agreement.

Down payment – The money you put "down" against the full purchase price of a property that is not included in the mortgage.

Due Diligence – The effort you put into investigating every consideration on a potential purchase.

Equity – The real dollar value of your property.

Escrow – Something of value (money or documents) that are held by a third party until all aspects of an agreement have been met.

Flip – Resale of a property very soon after purchase.

Grandfathered – Exempt from current laws, having been protected by previous laws.

Home Equity Line of Credit – A revolving credit account that uses the mortgage of your home as collateral. You may borrow none of the value to all of the value of the available credit available.

Interest – The price you pay for borrowing the money.

Leverage – Using borrowed money to increase your buying power

Lien – A claim against property or assets.

LTV – Loan to value ratio.

MAO – Maximum Allowable Offer

Mortgage – A written contract that establishes a lien against a property securing a debt.

Motivated Seller - A seller who is very interested in selling for any reason...death in the family, divorce, relocation, etc.

Net Return – Amount of money you realize after all expenses have been paid on a property.

Passive Income – Money coming in that you don't have to trade time for.

Passive income – money that you don't have to work for.

Point – One percent of a mortgage value.

Principle – The amount of the outstanding loan.

Refinance – Taking out a new loan against a property asset.

Refinance – Taking out a new loan against a property.

Rehab – Rehabilitation or renovation of an existing property.

Revenue – Money coming in to your account.

ROI – Return on investment.

Soft Market – Where there is a surplus of a commodity and a low demand for that commodity.

Turnaround – Bringing a rental that is not up to market rent up to market rent; often as the result of putting appropriate property management into place.

Walk Through – A physical inspection of a property you're purchasing just prior to closing.

Recommended Reading List

Many people have asked, "Jim, how did you do all this?" For me it all started when I picked up Napoleon Hill's book, *Think and Grow Rich.* Reading that book changed my world.

Charlie "TREMENDOUS" Jones said, "You will be the same person five years from now as you are today except for the books you read and the people you meet."

I made a decision to be a different person. My recommended reading list is constantly expanding. As of today, here are some of the books that helped me on my journey:

Albom, Mitch – *Tuesdays with Morrie: An Old Man, a Young Man and Life's Greatest Lessons, The Five People You Meet in Heaven*

Bartmann, Bill – *Billionaire Secrets to Success*

Brady, Shelly – *Ten Things I Learned from Bill Porter*

Brown, Les – *It's Not Over Until You Win*

Byrne, Rhonda - *The Secret*

Camp, Jim – *Start with NO*

Canfield, Jack – *Dare to Win*

Clason, George S. – *The Richest Man in Babylon*

Collins, Jim – *Good to Great*

Cousins, Norman – *Anatomy of an Illness*

Dennis, Felix – *How to Get Rich*

Eker, T. Harv – *Secrets of the Millionaire Mind*

Gitomer, Jeffrey – *The Sales Bible*

Haggai, John E. – *Paul J. Meyer and the Art of Giving*

Hill, Napoleon – *Think and Grow Rich, Positive Action Plan*

Hoffer, Eric – *The True Believer*

Jones, Charlie – *Life is Tremendous*

Keith, Kent M. – *Anyway: The Paradoxical Commandments*

Kennedy, Dan – *No B.S. Marketing to the Affluent, No B.S. Ruthless Management of People and Profits, No B.S. Direct Marketing, No B.S. Wealth Attraction for Entrepreneurs, No B.S. Sales Success, No B.S. Time Management for Entrepreneurs*

Kroc, Ray – *Grinding It Out: The Making of McDonalds*

Kushner, Harold S. – *Living a Life that Matters*

Landrum, Gene N. – *Profiles of Power and Success, The Superman Syndrome*

Lechter, Sharon – *Three Feet From Gold: Turn Your Obstacles into Opportunities*

Mandino, Og – *The Greatest Salesman in the World, A Better Way to Live, The Greatest Miracle in the World, The Greatest Secret in the World, Og Mandino's University of Success*

McKinney, Frank – *Burst This!, The Tap, Dead Fred, Flying Lunchboxes and the Good Luck Circle*

Mother Teresa – *A Simple Path*

Mulry John, - *Your Elephant's Under Threat, The Truth!*

Peters, Thomas J. – *In Search of Excellence*

Peters, Tom – *Re-Imagine!*

Philips, Bill – *Body for Life*

Proctor, Bob – *It's Not About The Money*

Robert, Cavett – *Success With People*

Rohn, Jim – *The Seasons of Life*

Stovall, Jim – *The Ultimate Gift*

Wilde, Stuart – *The Trick to Money is Having Some*

Wooden, John – *The Essential Wooden*

About the Author

Jim Toner has enjoyed a long career as a real estate investor, radio show host, speaker, and consultant.

He has spoken throughout the Country on the value of intelligent real estate investing and has appeared with the likes of Frank McKinney, Bill Bartmann, Sharon Lechter, The Napoleon Hill Foundation, and many more.

Jim's expertise in making real estate investment "user friendly" for the general public has put his services in very big demand. People routinely pay $2,000.00 to $25,000.00 and travel from all over the country to attend his real estate investment programs.

Jim is an accomplished entrepreneur who has been in the trenches of the real estate investment world for over 27 years having taught thousands the path towards financial freedom by using his custom, "12 little houses plan".

He is also an active philanthropist having been nationally recognized by his work with veterans and the homeless. He is an active member of Frank and Nilsa McKinney's Caring House Project Foundation as well the Advisory Board Chair of a Pittsburgh, Pennsylvania Salvation Army branch.

He currently works with a limited Private Client Group as well coaching groups both of which have waiting lists. He occasionally accepts new private coaching clients on investment real estate and entrepreneurial / business issues.

For information regarding Jim's programs, speaking engagements, or availability for consulting, visit:

www.creatingwealth101.com